REMBRANDT'S
LIFE OF
CHRIST

PAINTINGS, DRAWINGS, AND

ETCHINGS BY REMBRANDT, WITH

QUOTATIONS FROM THE GOSPELS

AND THE GOSPEL STORIES RETOLD

REMBRANDT'S LIFE OF CHRIST

BY OWEN S. RACHLEFF

ABRADALE PRESS, PUBLISHERS, NEW YORK

Library of Congress Catalog Card Number: 66-29135
Printed and bound in Japan.

CONTENTS

REMBRANDT'S LIFE OF CHRIST

PAINTINGS, DRAWINGS, AND ETCHINGS BY REMBRANDT

WITH QUOTATIONS FROM THE GOSPELS

vi

xi

xii

THE LIFE OF CHRIST

THE GOSPEL STORIES RETOLD
BY OWEN S. RACHLEFF

PREFACE

One of the first important paintings created by Rembrandt was a subject from the New Testament, *Judas Returning the Thirty Pieces of Silver* (page 84). Constantin Huygens, secretary to the Stadholder Prince, Frederick Henry, compared the quality of this work with that of any ancient or Italian master. That was in 1630, when Rembrandt was not yet twenty-five years old. Later, probably under Huygens' influence, Rembrandt received a commission to paint, for Prince Henry's chapel, a series of five scenes from the Passion of Christ, including *The Descent from the Cross* (page 99).

From then until his death in 1669, Rembrandt created over eight hundred Biblical subjects, even though religious art was decidedly unpopular in Calvinist Holland of the seventeenth century. In fact, religious paintings were entirely banned from Protestant churches, and artists were advised that they might paint such scenes only for their own diversion. Few chose to do so; most artists supported the flourishing Dutch tradition of genre art, portraiture, and landscape painting—all save Rembrandt. He stood practically alone as a religious artist, creating for himself a deeply personal and spiritual record of the Scriptures. Some perceptive critics and collectors of the time did indeed appreciate this Biblical work, and specially praised the artist's adherence to the holy text. But few commissioned him to create such Biblical paintings. Thus he worked in an unpopular and unprofitable field, despite the grave financial difficulties that beset his later life.

It was during such times of personal strife that Rembrandt drew closest to the New Testament as a source of artistic and spiritual inspiration, for he was a painter devoted to revealing the human condition, and was supremely able to fuse the human and divine characteristics of apparently ordinary scenes from the life of Christ. The Saviour himself was to be the focus of what Rembrandt called his search for "the deepest inward emotion." His portrait of Jesus (page 3) accordingly defies the religious strictures of his times, as well as the traditions of Baroque art; for here is the Saviour as a man—indeed a Semitic man—sallow in complexion, dark of hair, not unlike one of the many pious Jews whom Rembrandt saw every day near his house on the edge of the Jewish quarter in Amsterdam.

Other leading figures of the Gospels similarly come to life as real, everyday men in Rembrandt's art. In *The Denial of Peter* (page 83), the great Apostle—the rock upon whom Jesus laid the foundations of his Church—is seen with troubled eyes as he helplessly tries to parry the dangerous questions of his inquisitive companions.

Yet there is charm and tenderness, especially in the early scenes from the Gospels. *The Visitation* (page 6) is set *en famille,* with servants and neighbors bustling about as part of the drama. *The Angel Warns Joseph in a Dream* (page 25), though a scene of portent and mystery, also radiates holy peace and simplicity.

But it is God's forgiveness of repentant man, one of the greatest themes of the Gospels, that most succored Rembrandt during his difficult later life. *The Prodigal Son* particularly appealed to the artist in the context of his personal hardships, and he often drew or painted the highlights of this parable (pages 66 and 67). Moreover, the universal drama of Christ's Passion so inflamed the artist's vast sympathy that he included himself in *The Raising of the Cross* (page 94), where he is the troubled man in the blue cap, and in *The Descent from the Cross* (page 99), where he is the figure in blue who clutches Christ's lifeless arm.

Rembrandt's uncanny grasp of human reactions is no less vivid in the many drawings and etchings that appear in this book. St. Peter, realized in a few strokes of the pen, sits uneasily, almost fearfully, as Jesus kneels before him in *Christ Washing the Disciples' Feet* (page 78). Later, Jesus himself appears, numbed with inner conflict in spite of the angel's ministrations, in the etching *The Agony in the Garden* (page 80), which represents the essence of graphic facility and a high point of the etcher's art.

Along with Rembrandt's vision of the life of Christ, the four Gospels are here presented in a new, modern, and integrated narrative. It is hoped that from this text the reader will be moved to explore the Bible itself, with a clearer understanding of the events and themes related by the Evangelists. He will thereby realize, all the more, the great extent of Rembrandt's faithful adherence to the Gospels and the reverence he manifested through line, color, and light and shade, by brush stroke, pen point, and the etcher's needle. Truly, in Rembrandt's art, "Word was made flesh and dwelt among us."

O.S.R.

NOTE

The Biblical excerpts with the illustrations are derived from the Authorized King James Version of the Holy Bible. In order to present a smooth-flowing narrative from picture to picture and, above all, to emphasize the specific details of Rembrandt's illustrations, the passages have necessarily been somewhat abridged.

In addition, because Rembrandt often explored many aspects of the same Biblical story, there will be several treatments of certain subjects, in order to show the artist's various interpretations of one theme. For dramatic emphasis, in many cases, only the central narrative portions of the paintings, drawings, and etchings have been selected.

REMBRANDT'S
LIFE OF
CHRIST

REMBRANDT'S
LIFE OF

CHRIST

The Angel Gabriel is Sent unto Mary

AND THE ANGEL CAME IN UNTO HER, AND SAID, HAIL THOU THAT ART HIGHLY FAVORED, THE LORD IS WITH THEE: BLESSED ART THOU AMONG WOMEN.

AND THE ANGEL SAID UNTO HER, FEAR NOT, MARY: FOR THOU HAST FOUND FAVOR WITH GOD. AND, BEHOLD, THOU SHALT CONCEIVE IN THY WOMB, AND BRING FORTH A SON, AND SHALT CALL HIS NAME **JESUS.**

D.2618.

Mary Visits Her Cousin Elisabeth

MARY AROSE AND ENTERED INTO THE HOUSE

OF ZACHARIAS, AND SALUTED ELISABETH.

The Visitation. *Oil on panel*

ELISABETH WAS FILLED WITH THE HOLY GHOST...
AND SAID, BLESSED ART THOU AMONG WOMEN.

The Naming of John the Baptist. *Drawing*

Zacharias Names His Son

AND HE ASKED FOR A WRITING TABLE, AND
WROTE, SAYING, HIS NAME IS JOHN ... AND
THOU, CHILD, SHALT BE CALLED THE
PROPHET OF THE HIGHEST: FOR THOU SHALT
GO BEFORE THE FACE OF THE LORD TO
PREPARE HIS WAYS....

AND THERE WERE IN THE SAME COUNTRY
SHEPHERDS ABIDING IN THE FIELD,
KEEPING WATCH OVER THEIR FLOCK BY
NIGHT.

AND, LO, THE ANGEL OF THE LORD CAME
UPON THEM, AND THE GLORY OF THE LORD
SHONE ROUND ABOUT THEM....

AND THE ANGEL SAID UNTO THEM, FEAR NOT:
FOR, BEHOLD, I BRING YOU GOOD TIDINGS
OF GREAT JOY, WHICH SHALL BE TO ALL
PEOPLE.

The Angel Appearing to the Shepherds. *Drawing*

The Adoration of the Shepherds

THE SHEPHERDS SAID ONE TO ANOTHER, LET US NOW GO EVEN UNTO BETHLEHEM, AND SEE THIS THING WHICH IS COME TO PASS....

AND THEY CAME WITH HASTE, AND FOUND MARY AND JOSEPH, AND THE BABE LYING IN A MANGER.

The Adoration of the Shepherds. *Oil on canvas*

Mary and Joseph Present Jesus in the Temple

WHEN EIGHT DAYS WERE
ACCOMPLISHED FOR THE
CIRCUMCISING OF THE CHILD...
THEY BROUGHT HIM TO
JERUSALEM, TO PRESENT HIM
TO THE LORD...AND
TO OFFER A SACRIFICE....

The Circumcision. *Oil on canvas*

Simeon in the Temple

AND, BEHOLD, THERE WAS A MAN IN JERUSALEM,

WHOSE NAME WAS SIMEON ... THEN HE TOOK

THE CHILD UP IN HIS ARMS, AND BLESSED GOD,

LEFT: The Presentation in the Temple. *Oil on panel*   ABOVE: The Presentation in the Temple. *Etching*

Simeon's Prayer

AND SAID,

LORD, NOW LETTEST THOU

THY SERVANT DEPART

IN PEACE...FOR MINE EYES

HAVE SEEN THY SALVATION....

20

The Infancy of Jesus

JOSEPH AND MARY MARVELED AT
THOSE THINGS WHICH WERE SPOKEN
OF THE CHILD.

NOW WHEN JESUS WAS

BORN IN BETHLEHEM . . .

The Holy Family with Angels. *Oil on canvas*

ABOVE: The Adoration of the Magi. *Drawing*   RIGHT: The Adoration of the Magi. *Oil on panel*

The Visit of the Wise Men

THERE CAME WISE MEN FROM THE EAST TO JERUSALEM, SAYING, WHERE IS HE THAT IS BORN KING OF THE JEWS?

Joseph's Dream

AND WHEN THEY WERE DEPARTED,
BEHOLD, THE ANGEL OF THE LORD
APPEARETH TO JOSEPH IN A DREAM,
SAYING, ARISE, AND TAKE THE
YOUNG CHILD AND HIS MOTHER, AND
FLEE INTO EGYPT...FOR HEROD
WILL SEEK THE YOUNG CHILD TO
DESTROY HIM.

Joseph Takes Mary and Jesus to Egypt

HE TOOK THE YOUNG CHILD AND HIS MOTHER BY NIGHT, AND DEPARTED INTO EGYPT: AND WAS THERE UNTIL THE DEATH OF HEROD....

LEFT: The Flight into Egypt. *Oil on panel*   BELOW: The Flight into Egypt: The Holy Family Crossing a Brook. *Etching*

LEFT: The Holy Family with Cat. *Etching*

BELOW: The Holy Family. *Drawing*

RIGHT: The Holy Family. *Oil on panel*

The Holy Family
Returns to Israel

AND HE AROSE,

AND TOOK THE

YOUNG CHILD

AND HIS MOTHER,

AND CAME INTO

THE LAND OF ISRAEL . . .

AND DWELT IN A CITY CALLED NAZARETH. . . .

Jesus and His Parents Visit the Temple

AND WHEN HE WAS TWELVE YEARS OLD… THEY FOUND HIM IN THE TEMPLE, SITTING IN THE MIDST OF THE DOCTORS, BOTH HEARING THEM, AND ASKING THEM QUESTIONS.

BELOW: Christ Among the Doctors. *Etching*   ABOVE RIGHT: Christ Among the Doctors. *Etching*   BELOW RIGHT: Christ Among the Doctors. *Drawing*

Jesus Between His Parents, Returning from Jerusalem. *Etching*

The Holy Family Returns Home

AND HE WENT DOWN WITH THEM, AND CAME
TO NAZARETH...

AND JESUS INCREASED IN WISDOM AND STATURE,
AND IN FAVOR WITH GOD AND MAN.

The Preaching of John the Baptist

THE WORD OF GOD CAME UNTO JOHN THE
SON OF ZACHARIAS IN THE WILDERNESS.
AND HE CAME INTO ALL THE COUNTRY
ABOUT JORDAN, PREACHING THE BAPTISM
OF REPENTANCE FOR THE REMISSION
OF SINS. . . .

The Baptism of Jesus

THEN COMETH JESUS FROM GALILEE
TO JORDAN UNTO JOHN, TO BE BAPTIZED
OF HIM.

AND, LO, THE HEAVENS WERE OPENED
UNTO HIM . . . AND, LO, A VOICE FROM HEAVEN,
SAYING, THIS IS MY BELOVED SON, IN
WHOM I AM WELL PLEASED.

Christ Baptized in the Jordan. *Drawing*

THEN WAS JESUS LED UP OF THE SPIRIT
INTO THE WILDERNESS TO BE TEMPTED
OF THE DEVIL.

AND THE DEVIL TAKETH HIM UP INTO
AN EXCEEDING HIGH MOUNTAIN, AND
SHOWETH HIM ALL THE KINGDOMS OF
THE WORLD ... AND SAITH UNTO HIM, ALL
THESE THINGS WILL I GIVE THEE, IF THOU
WILT FALL DOWN AND WORSHIP ME.

THEN SAITH JESUS UNTO HIM, GET THEE
HENCE, SATAN. . . .

Christ Calls the Apostles Simon and Andrew. *Drawing*

NOW AS HE WALKED BY THE SEA OF GALILEE, HE

SAW SIMON AND ANDREW HIS BROTHER CASTING

Jesus Calls

His Disciples

The Miraculous Draught of Fishes. *Drawing*

A NET INTO THE SEA. . . . AND HE SAITH UNTO THEM,

FOLLOW ME, AND I WILL MAKE YOU FISHERS OF MEN.

AND THERE CAME A LEPER TO HIM, BESEECHING HIM, AND KNEELING DOWN TO HIM, AND SAYING

Christ Healing a Leper. *Drawing*

UNTO HIM, IF THOU WILT, THOU CANST MAKE

ME CLEAN. AND JESUS PUT FORTH HIS HAND. . . .

Christ Healing a Leper. *Drawing*

Jesus and Nicodemus

THERE WAS A MAN OF THE PHARISEES,
NAMED NICODEMUS, A RULER OF THE JEWS....

AND JESUS SAID UNTO HIM...FOR GOD SO
LOVED THE WORLD, THAT HE GAVE HIS ONLY
BEGOTTEN SON, THAT WHOSOEVER BELIEVETH
IN HIM SHOULD NOT PERISH, BUT HAVE
EVERLASTING LIFE.

Christ and Nicodemus. *Drawing*

Jesus in Samaria

THEN COMETH HE TO A CITY OF SAMARIA...
THERE COMETH A WOMAN OF SAMARIA TO
DRAW WATER....

THE WOMAN SAITH UNTO HIM, I KNOW THAT
MESSIAS COMETH, WHICH IS CALLED
CHRIST... AND JESUS SAITH UNTO HER, I THAT
SPEAK UNTO THEE AM HE.

Christ and the Samaritan Woman. *Oil on panel*

Jesus Calls the Apostles

HE CALLED UNTO HIM HIS DISCIPLES:
AND OF THEM HE CHOSE TWELVE, WHOM
ALSO HE NAMED APOSTLES. . . .

AND HE TAUGHT THEM, SAYING . . .

AFTER THIS MANNER THEREFORE PRAY YE:

OUR FATHER WHICH ART IN HEAVEN,

HALLOWED BE THY NAME. . . .

Jesus and His Disciples. *Drawing*

NOW WHEN HE HAD ENDED ALL
HIS SAYINGS IN THE AUDIENCE
OF THE PEOPLE, HE ENTERED
INTO CAPERNAUM. AND A
CERTAIN CENTURION'S SERVANT,
WHO WAS DEAR UNTO HIM, WAS
SICK, AND READY TO DIE.

AND THEY THAT WERE SENT,
RETURNING TO THE HOUSE,
FOUND THE SERVANT WHOLE
THAT HAD BEEN SICK.

The Centurion Kneeling Before Christ. *Drawing*

The Woman Taken in Adultery

AND THE SCRIBES AND PHARISEES
BROUGHT UNTO HIM A WOMAN TAKEN
IN ADULTERY....

JESUS STOOPED DOWN, AND WITH HIS
FINGER WROTE ON THE GROUND....
AND SAID UNTO THEM, HE THAT IS
WITHOUT SIN AMONG YOU, LET HIM
FIRST CAST A STONE AT HER.

ABOVE: The Woman Taken in Adultery. *Drawing*   **RIGHT:** The Woman Taken in Adultery. *Oil on panel*

Christ Preaching Before the Pharisees. *Drawing*

Jesus Makes a Speech to the Pharisees

WHEN THE PHARISEES HEARD IT, THEY SAID,

THIS FELLOW DOTH NOT CAST OUT DEVILS....

AND HE CALLED UNTO THEM...

O GENERATION OF VIPERS....

Jesus on the Sea of Galilee

NOW IT CAME TO PASS ON A CERTAIN DAY,
THAT HE WENT INTO A SHIP WITH HIS
DISCIPLES. . . .

AND THERE CAME DOWN A STORM OF WIND
ON THE LAKE. . . .

AND THEY CAME TO HIM, AND AWOKE
HIM, SAYING, MASTER, MASTER, WE
PERISH. . . .

The Storm on the Sea of Galilee. *Oil on canvas*

ABOVE: Christ and the Ailing Woman. *Drawing*

ABOVE RIGHT: The Raising of the Daughter of Jairus. *Drawing*

BELOW RIGHT: Christ Walking on Water. *Drawing*

Healing the Sick

AND JESUS WENT ABOUT ALL THE
CITIES AND VILLAGES . . . HEALING
EVERY SICKNESS AND EVERY
DISEASE AMONG THE PEOPLE.

ABOVE: The Good Samaritan. *Drawing*

RIGHT: The Good Samaritan at the Inn. *Drawing*

A Good Samaritan

Helps a Wounded Man

The Good Samaritan at the Inn. *Oil on canvas*

A CERTAIN SAMARITAN . . . CAME WHERE HE WAS: AND WHEN HE SAW HIM, HE HAD COMPASSION ON HIM. . . . AND BROUGHT HIM TO AN INN, AND TOOK CARE OF HIM.

A Blind Man is Healed

AS JESUS PASSED BY, HE SAW A MAN WHICH WAS BLIND FROM HIS BIRTH... AND HE ANOINTED THE EYES OF THE BLIND MAN... AND SAID UNTO HIM, GO, WASH IN THE POOL OF SILOAM....

Christ Healing a Blind Man. *Drawing*

Lazarus of Bethany is Raised from the Dead

AND JESUS LIFTED UP HIS EYES, AND...

HE CRIED WITH A LOUD VOICE, LAZARUS,

COME FORTH. AND HE THAT WAS DEAD

CAME FORTH....

The Raising of Lazarus. *Etching*

The Raising of Lazarus. *Oil on panel*

RIGHT: The Departure of the Prodigal Son. *Drawing*

BELOW: The Prodigal Son with Loose Women. *Drawing*

Jesus Tells the Parable of the Prodigal Son

AND HE SAID, THE YOUNGER SON ... WASTED HIS SUBSTANCE WITH RIOTOUS LIVING ....

ON FOLLOWING PAGES:

TOP LEFT: The Parable of the Talents. *Drawing*

BOTTOM LEFT: The Parable of the King Who
Took Account of His Servants. *Drawing*

TOP RIGHT: The Parable of the
Laborers in the Vineyard. *Drawing*

BOTTOM RIGHT: Christ Conversing
with Martha and Mary. *Drawing*

LEFT: The Return of the Prodigal Son. *Oil on canvas*

BELOW: The Return of the Prodigal Son. *Etching*

AND WHEN HE CAME TO
HIMSELF, HE SAID ... I WILL
ARISE AND GO TO MY
FATHER, AND WILL SAY UNTO
HIM, FATHER, I HAVE SINNED ....

Jesus the
Teacher

AND HE SPAKE A PARABLE UNTO THEM...

AND HE ENTERED INTO A CERTAIN

VILLAGE: AND A CERTAIN WOMAN NAMED
MARTHA RECEIVED HIM INTO HER HOUSE.

*John the Baptist
is Beheaded*

AND THE KING

SENT AN

EXECUTIONER...

AND HE WENT

AND BEHEADED

HIM IN THE

PRISON.

The Beheading of John the Baptist. *Drawing*

Cleansing the Temple

AND JESUS WENT INTO THE TEMPLE OF GOD . . . .
AND OVERTHREW THE TABLES OF THE MONEY-
CHANGERS . . . .

Jesus in the Temple

AND THE BLIND AND THE LAME CAME TO HIM
IN THE TEMPLE; AND HE HEALED THEM.

LEFT: Christ Driving the Money-Changers from the Temple. *Etching*   ABOVE: Christ Healing the Sick ("The Hundred Guilder Print"). *Etching*   *73*

ABOVE: Christ Preaching ("La Petite Tombe"). *Etching*   RIGHT: The Parable of the Unworthy Wedding Guest. *Drawing*

Jesus Preaches

MY HOUSE SHALL BE CALLED

THE HOUSE OF PRAYER....

THE KINGDOM OF HEAVEN IS LIKE UNTO A
CERTAIN KING, WHICH MADE A MARRIAGE FOR
HIS SON, AND SENT FORTH HIS SERVANTS TO
CALL THEM THAT WERE BIDDEN TO THE
WEDDING: AND THEY WOULD NOT COME...FOR
MANY ARE CALLED, BUT FEW ARE CHOSEN.

The Pharisees Attempt to Entangle Jesus

TELL US THEREFORE, WHAT THINKEST THOU? IS IT LAWFUL TO GIVE TRIBUTE UNTO CAESAR, OR NOT?...

THEN SAITH HE UNTO THEM, RENDER THEREFORE UNTO CAESAR THE THINGS WHICH ARE CAESAR'S....

The Tribute Money. *Oil on panel*

Jesus at the Last Supper

AND THEY MADE READY THE PASSOVER...
AND HE POURETH WATER, AND BEGAN TO
WASH THE DISCIPLES' FEET....

ABOVE: Christ Washing the Disciples' Feet. *Drawing*   RIGHT: The Last Supper. *Drawing after Leonardo da Vinci*

WHEN JESUS HAD THUS SAID, HE WAS
TROUBLED IN SPIRIT, AND SAID, VERILY,
VERILY, I SAY UNTO YOU, THAT ONE
OF YOU SHALL BETRAY ME.

LEFT: The Agony in the Garden. *Etching*

BELOW: Christ Awakening the Apostles
on the Mount of Olives. *Drawing*

RIGHT: The Arrest of Christ. *Drawing*

AND THERE APPEARED AN ANGEL UNTO HIM

FROM HEAVEN, STRENGTHENING HIM...

THEN CAME THEY, AND LAID HANDS ON

JESUS, AND TOOK HIM.

THEN THE BAND AND THE CAPTAIN AND OFFICERS... TOOK JESUS, AND BOUND HIM, AND LED HIM AWAY TO ANNAS....

LEFT: Christ Before Annas. *Drawing*

RIGHT: The Denial of Peter. *Oil on canvas*

BELOW RIGHT: The Repentant Peter. *Etching*

Peter Denies the Lord

AGAIN HE DENIED IT . . . AND THE
COCK CREW . . . AND HE WENT
OUT AND WEPT BITTERLY.

83

Judas Repents

His Betrayal

THEN JUDAS ...

REPENTED HIMSELF,

Judas Returning the Thirty Pieces of Silver. *Oil on wood*

AND BROUGHT AGAIN THE THIRTY PIECES

OF SILVER TO THE CHIEF PRIESTS.... 85

Jesus Before Pilate

AND WHEN THEY HAD
BOUND HIM ... THEY
DELIVERED HIM TO
PONTIUS PILATE ...
AND PILATE SAITH
UNTO THEM, I FIND
NO FAULT IN HIM ....

LEFT: Christ Before Pilate. *Oil on canvas*

RIGHT: Christ Before Pilate. *Etching*

Pilate Washes His Hands

WHEN PILATE SAW THAT HE COULD PREVAIL
NOTHING . . . HE TOOK WATER, AND WASHED HIS
HANDS BEFORE THE MULTITUDE, SAYING, I
AM INNOCENT OF THE BLOOD OF THIS JUST
PERSON . . . .

Pilate Washing His Hands. *Oil on canvas*

Jesus is Mocked

THEN CAME JESUS FORTH, WEARING THE CROWN
OF THORNS, AND THE PURPLE ROBE. AND
PILATE SAITH UNTO THEM, BEHOLD THE MAN!

LEFT:

Christ at the Column. *Oil on canvas*

ABOVE:

The Mocking of Christ. *Drawing*

RIGHT:

Ecce Homo ("Christ Before the People").

Etching

Jesus at Golgotha

AND HE BEARING HIS CROSS WENT FORTH INTO A PLACE CALLED ... GOLGOTHA. AND THERE FOLLOWED HIM A GREAT COMPANY OF PEOPLE, AND OF WOMEN, WHICH ALSO BEWAILED AND LAMENTED HIM.

IT WAS THE THIRD HOUR

LEFT: Christ Carrying the Cross. *Drawing*

RIGHT: The Raising of the Cross. *Drawing*

LEFT: The Raising of the Cross.

Oil on canvas

RIGHT: Christ Crucified Between the Two Thieves ("The Three Crosses").

Etching

BELOW: Calvary. *Drawing*

AND
THEY
CRUCIFIED
HIM.

LEFT: The Crucifixion. *Oil on Wood*

ABOVE: Christ Crucified Between the

Two Thieves: Christ Offered a Sponge. *Drawing*

LEFT: The Crucifixion: The Blow of the Lance. *Drawing*

97

LEFT: The Descent from the Cross: Removal of the Nails. *Etching*

BELOW: The Descent from the Cross. *Etching*

RIGHT: The Descent from the Cross. *Oil on panel*

The Deposition of Jesus' Body

AND AFTER THIS JOSEPH
OF ARIMATHEA ... BESOUGHT
PILATE THAT HE MIGHT TAKE
AWAY THE BODY OF JESUS ....

Joseph of Arimathea Prepares Jesus' Body

AND HE BOUGHT FINE LINEN, AND TOOK HIM DOWN, AND WRAPPED HIM IN THE LINEN....

LEFT: The Lamentation over Christ. *Drawing*   ABOVE: Lamentation. *Drawing*

The Burial

AND LAID HIM
IN A SEPULCHRE
WHICH WAS HEWN
OUT OF A ROCK.

RIGHT: Christ Carried to the Tomb. *Etching*

BELOW: The Entombment. *Drawing*

The Entombment. *Oil on canvas*

AND MARY MAGDALENE AND MARY THE MOTHER
OF JOSES BEHELD WHERE HE WAS LAID.

The Resurrection

AND WHEN THE SABBATH
WAS PAST...BEHOLD,
THERE WAS A GREAT
EARTHQUAKE: FOR THE
ANGEL OF THE LORD
DESCENDED...HIS
COUNTENANCE WAS LIKE
LIGHTNING, AND HIS
RAIMENT WHITE AS SNOW....

The First Appearance of Christ

NOW WHEN JESUS WAS RISEN
EARLY THE FIRST DAY OF THE WEEK,
HE APPEARED FIRST TO MARY
MAGDALENE... AND SAID UNTO HER,
TOUCH ME NOT; FOR I AM NOT YET
ASCENDED TO MY FATHER....

LEFT: Christ on the Road
to Emmaus. *Drawing*

RIGHT: Christ at Emmaus.
Oil on panel

*Jesus
at Emmaus*

AFTER THAT HE APPEARED...IN A VILLAGE
CALLED EMMAUS...AND IT CAME TO PASS,
AS HE SAT AT MEAT...THEY KNEW HIM;
AND HE VANISHED OUT OF THEIR SIGHT.

Doubting Thomas

BUT HE SAID UNTO THEM, EXCEPT I SHALL
SEE IN HIS HANDS THE PRINT OF THE
NAILS...I WILL NOT BELIEVE...THEN CAME
JESUS...THEN SAITH HE TO THOMAS, REACH
HITHER THY FINGER, AND BEHOLD MY HANDS....

LEFT: The Incredulity of Thomas. *Drawing*   ABOVE: The Incredulity of Thomas. *Drawing*

The Ascension

SO THEN, AFTER THE LORD HAD SPOKEN
UNTO THEM, HE WAS RECEIVED UP
INTO HEAVEN, AND SAT ON THE RIGHT
HAND OF GOD.

THE GOSPEL
STORIES RETOLD

In order to relate these stories to Rembrandt's work, and to the Biblical quotations, the paintings, drawings, and etchings illustrating the preceding section of this book are here reproduced again.

Head of Christ
Oil on panel

1.

THE ANNUNCIATION

ONE DAY in spring, the angel Gabriel appeared in the city of Nazareth, in the hills of Galilee. There lived the maiden Mary, who was betrothed to Joseph, the carpenter.

It was a peaceful day. Mary was seated quietly in her house, reading her prayers.

"Hail," the angel said to her. "The Lord is with thee; among all women art thou most blessed."

Mary humbly lowered her eyes, for she did not understand. Then Gabriel prophesied that Mary would soon give birth to a son—the Hope of the World—and that this son would be called Joshua, or, as we know him, Jesus.

"He shall be great," said the angel, "and he shall be called the Son of the Highest; and the Lord God shall give unto him the throne of his father, King David. And he shall reign for ever and ever, and unto his kingdom there shall be no end."

Mary bowed her head and replied:

"Whatever the Lord God commands, I will gladly do."

Then Gabriel disappeared, and Mary remained at her prayers in the quiet of her room.

The Annunciation
Drawing

2.

THE VISITATION

ELISABETH, THE WIFE of Zacharias, was Mary's cousin. She sent word to the younger woman that, by a miracle of God, she was expecting a son. Mary had been told by Gabriel that Elisabeth would so conceive, and she was overjoyed.

Filled with the Spirit of God, Mary journeyed to her cousin's home for a visit. When Elisabeth saw her, she was stirred by Mary's beauty and serenity, and she said:

"Surely you are blessed among all women and blessed is the fruit of your womb."

Mary lifted her voice in thanks to God for her great fortune.

"My soul magnifies the Lord," she said, "for He has blessed me. And though I be humble, all generations from this time forth will call me blessed, for there is no single thing that the Lord cannot do."

Mary stayed with her cousin Elisabeth for three months, and the two women often talked of the wonders of God and His blessings upon the Children of Israel.

Then Mary returned to Nazareth and wed Joseph the carpenter.

The Visitation
Oil on panel

Though he was a humble man in a humble trade, Joseph was descended from the royal house of King David. He too was visited by an angel in a dream and was told of the wonderful child that Mary was to bear. Being a pious Jew, Joseph was overjoyed to know that the prophecy of Isaiah would be fulfilled, for it said that a Saviour would be born to the family of the House of David in the city of David and that the birth would be like no other in all the world.

3.

THE ADVENT OF JOHN

NOW ELISABETH was about to give birth. Many friends and relatives gathered in the house of Zacharias to celebrate the great event.

"What will they name the child?" the neighbors wondered.

"Zacharias, of course," one man said. "It is the custom to name first-born sons after their fathers."

But Elisabeth interrupted, and announced:

"My husband wishes the boy to bear another name that an angel

The Naming of John the Baptist
Drawing

told him long ago. But, since he has lost his speech, we do not know what that name will be."

Zacharias was listening. He beckoned the guests to his side and then with his pen he wrote the name *John* on his writing table. And, in the same instant, his speech returned.

"John shall be his name," said the father joyously.

And filled with the Spirit of God, Zacharias prophesied:

"This child named John will be the forerunner of the Highest One whom God will send to save the world."

Young John grew into manhood, and was filled with great religious fervor. Later, when he was about thirty years old, he went into the desert of Judea and lived alone, wearing a rough coat of camel's hair and eating only locusts and honey. His beard grew long, and his eyes shone with inspiration. Thus, when he appeared in public, he frightened many people, as Elijah had frightened the wicked Ahab years before. John's message was also strange and foreboding:

"Repent!" he cried. "For the Kingdom of Heaven is at hand!"

Because of his zeal, many thought that John was the Messiah. But the strange prophet always disclaimed that great distinction.

"I am not worthy to untie the laces of His sandals," he would say. "I am only His prophet, and I lead the way."

Nevertheless, hundreds of Jews, seeking comfort from their sorrows, followed John and joined him in the worship of God. To purify their souls and refresh their spirits, John instructed them to immerse themselves in the cold, clear waters of the Jordan. This was the act of baptism, and, as a result, people called the prophet of the Lord John the Baptist.

4.

THE BIRTH OF JESUS

THE PROPHECY of the angel Gabriel was about to be fulfilled, for Mary was soon to bear her son, the infant Jesus. At this same time, a decree went out from Caesar Augustus, the Emperor of Rome, that each man in Judea was to return to the city of his birth so that a census might be taken.

Joseph the carpenter had been born in Bethlehem, a small city some distance from the town of Nazareth, where he and Mary lived. Obedient to the emperor's decree, Joseph gently placed Mary on a donkey and began the long journey to his childhood home.

When they reached Bethlehem, they found the city crowded and bustling with people, all of whom had come in answer to the emperor's decree. Joseph was concerned, for Mary was close to the time of her delivery, and he went from place to place, seeking shelter. But there was no room for them in the public places.

At one inn the owner told Joseph:

"You may stay in the stable tonight."

So Joseph led his wife into the stable among the horses, the sheep, and all the other gentle creatures. There she gave birth to her son and wrapped him in swaddling clothes and—lacking a cradle—she laid him in a feeding trough, called a manger. Thus was Jesus born.

Not far away, in the peaceful hills, certain shepherds were tending their flocks, when suddenly they saw a glowing angel appear.

"Fear not," he called to them, "for behold, I bring you good tidings

The Angel Appearing
to the Shepherds
Drawing

121

of great joy, which shall be to all people. For unto you is born this day in the city of David, which is Bethlehem, a Saviour; Christ the Lord. And this shall be a sign unto you; you shall find the baby wrapped in swaddling clothes, and lying in a manger."

The shepherds rejoiced. At last the long awaited prophecy was at hand and, as they rushed toward Bethlehem to see the newborn child, a brilliant new star shone in the deep black night, and a multitude of heavenly voices exclaimed:

"Glory to God in the highest and on earth peace, good will toward all men."

5.

THE ADORATION OF THE SHEPHERDS

LIKE A BEACON, steady and bright, the star of Bethlehem pointed the way to the stable where Mary and the baby were sleeping. Joseph watched over them in the light of a little fire he had kindled. How beautiful was the child and how peaceful was the night! The cows, sheep, and the other gentle creatures in the barn neither moved nor made a noise to disturb the mother and child.

Then, outside, quietly and reverently, the shepherds approached the barn, and saw the infant resting in the manger as the angel had described him. Kneeling, they prayed to God and gave thanks for the hope that was now in their hearts. This was the world's first Christmas.

For some time after, Mary and Joseph stayed in the stable caring for the newborn child. Then, after Jesus was circumcised, they journeyed to Jerusalem, so that the baby Jesus might be presented in the

The Adoration of
the Shepherds
Oil on canvas

The Circumcision
Oil on canvas

The Presentation
in the Temple
Oil on panel

The Presentation
in the Temple
Etching

Simeon in the Temple
Oil on panel

Temple. It was the custom in those days for a first-born Jewish son to be blessed by the priests while his father made the proper sacrifices to God. Joseph obeyed this law, and offered a pair of turtledoves, or pigeons, upon the sacred altar.

6.

SIMEON AND ANNA IN THE TEMPLE

WHILE JOSEPH AND MARY were thus in the Temple with their son, an old man named Simeon was praying off in a corner of the building. Every day, he came to pray for the Messiah, believing that he would not die until he had beheld the Saviour of the world. Now, as Simeon prayed, he lifted his head and saw Mary carrying Jesus from the altar. Immediately he knew that this was the Holy Child, and he approached Mary and said:

"This child is to be our Saviour. I know it in my heart. Therefore, I pray, let me hold him for a moment, so that I may depart in peace knowing my salvation."

Mary was very kind. She placed her baby in the old man's arms. An aged widow, Anna, also fondled the child, and the two elderly people had tears of happiness in their eyes.

All the while, Mary was somewhat puzzled. She remembered the

The Holy Family
with Angels
Oil on canvas

123

angel Gabriel and the wonderful things he had said about her child. Yet she wondered; how would this little baby be the Saviour of the world? Did God intend the Messiah to be like everyone else, to be born like a man, to grow up and go to school and to do all the things that other men do? Mary could not answer. Taking her child from Simeon, she returned with Joseph to Bethlehem.

7.

THE VISIT OF THE THREE KINGS

FAR TO THE EAST of Judea, there were three kingdoms ruled by three wise men. One king was fair, with golden hair; the second was ruddy, with a long gray beard; and the third was golden brown, with deep black curls upon his head. They had seen the wonderful star of Bethlehem, and they knew that the Messiah had been born.

So they gathered up many fine gifts and treasures and set out for Judea. All the while, they followed the brilliant star. But, when they came to the gates of Jerusalem, they could not be sure if the star pointed in that direction or just slightly beyond.

"We will ask King Herod," they said.

Herod had not heard about the newborn child. When the three wise men came before him they asked:

"Where may we find the new king of Israel, so that we may pay him homage?"

The wise men referred to Jesus as a king, not in the sense of one who sits upon an earthly throne, but as a king of goodness and peace. Herod did not understand this. He became immediately fearful that some child had been born who would one day take away his power. But he did not show his fear. Craftily, he called the three wise men to him and said:

"The prophets have written that this child would be born in Bethlehem, which is very near. Go there and find that child; then send word where he is, so that I may follow and pay my respects."

Herod had no intentions of paying his respects to the newborn king. In fact, it was his plan to murder Jesus as soon as he found where he lived.

The wise men did not suspect Herod of such an evil plan, and departed toward Bethlehem. Above them, the star shone brightly, ever leading the way to the barn where Mary and Joseph watched over the baby.

"Here at last is the place," said the wise men.

They loaded their arms with wonderful gifts, and came before Mary and Joseph and the child. For some time, they paid homage to the infant Jesus and placed their precious treasures at his feet. Then they planned to return to Herod with the news of Jesus' whereabouts. But as they slept that night, an angel appeared to each of them in a dream and warned them of Herod's plan. Quickly, the wise men packed their horses and left the land of Judea, so that Herod could not find them.

That same night, an angel appeared to Joseph and said:

"There is danger here. Take Mary and the baby, and flee into Egypt, for Herod means to murder the child."

The Adoration
of the Magi
Oil on panel

The Adoration
of the Magi
Drawing

The Angel Warns
Joseph in a Dream
Oil on panel

The Flight into Egypt
Oil on panel

Indeed, King Herod was filled with wrath, for the wise men had not returned, and the baby's whereabouts still remained unknown to him. He then conceived a terrible plan.

"I must find this child and destroy him," he thought. "If every baby under two years of age is killed, then surely this child will be among them."

So he ordered his soldiers to slaughter hundreds of innocent children in Bethlehem. By this time, however, Jesus was safely on his way to Egypt in the arms of his mother.

There, in Egypt, the Holy Family stayed for a time. Then word came that the evil Herod was dead. Joseph knew he could safely return to Judea. But, instead of going to Bethlehem, Joseph led his family north to the hills of Galilee and the town of Nazareth, where he and Mary had lived before. Thus, they avoided Herod's son, who was now the king in Jerusalem and who was just as wicked as his father had been.

The Flight into Egypt:
The Holy Family
Crossing a Brook
Etching

8.

JESUS AS A BOY

IN NAZARETH, Joseph followed his trade as a carpenter. His shop was next to the house where Mary and the baby Jesus spent the day. But, as Jesus grew up, it came time for him to learn his father's trade. Often, he would help Joseph at the carpenter's bench, planing wood and mending chairs.

Besides learning a trade, Jesus went to school. Every Jewish boy was obliged to learn the Torah, or the Five Books of Moses, so that he might

The Holy Family
with Cat
Etching

The Holy Family
Oil on panel

The Holy Family
Drawing

fully obey the laws of God. Jesus found this training very easy. Time after time, he was far ahead of the other boys in his lessons.

On the Sabbath and on holidays, Jesus and Joseph went to the synagogue in Nazareth to pray and study. Once again, Jesus proved most learned and devout. When he was twelve years old, his parents decided to take him to Jerusalem for the Passover festival.

Jesus had been in Jerusalem as a tiny baby, but he remembered nothing of the great city and the awesome Temple. Now, for the first time, he gazed upon the place that had been home to King David and King Solomon. His heart was filled with the love of God.

Many times before, the boy Jesus had felt a strong passion for God and for religion. But it seems that he was not yet aware of his role in the world. From what we know, neither Mary nor Joseph, nor any of the angels of God came to him and told him, "You are the Saviour." It was Jesus' task to learn this himself, as he lived and suffered like any other man. Nevertheless, by the time he was twelve, he *had* discovered one most important truth: that all good men might call themselves the sons of God and live a perfect and righteous life by doing as God would do if He Himself lived on earth.

In Jerusalem, Jesus spent little time at the festivities. Instead, he went to the Temple, and entered the study rooms where many learned rabbis and aged doctors sat conversing and discussing the Law. To their amazement, this mere youth of twelve seemed quite well versed in the

Christ Among
the Doctors
Etching

Christ Among
the Doctors
Etching

Christ Among
the Doctors
Drawing

teachings of Moses. After a while they sat in surprise as he instructed them on the deeper meanings and the inner truths of what he knew in his heart.

Mary and Joseph did not know that Jesus was in the Temple conversing with the rabbis and doctors. Nervously, they searched for him in the streets where the other boys were playing. But he could not be found. Nightfall was coming.

"Let us look in the Temple," said Joseph wearily.

There in the midst of the learned men, sat Jesus, discussing the most difficult points of religion.

"How worried we were," his mother said to him. "We did not know where to find you."

128

Jesus Between His Parents,
Returning from Jerusalem
Etching

Jesus was surprised.

"Where else should I be," he said, "but in my Father's house, attending to His business?"

Mary was puzzled. She did not understand that Jesus referred to God as his father and had meant no insult to Joseph. The three returned silently to Nazareth. For many years Jesus led a quiet life, studying, growing wise, and every day coming nearer to the truth of his great identity.

9.

THE BAPTISM OF JESUS

John the Baptist
Preaching
Oil on canvas

WHILE JESUS WAS GROWING to manhood, John the Baptist continued to preach in the desert. Time after time, he would pour the holy waters of the Jordan over the heads of people who were seeking comfort and help. Each time, he would announce the coming of One greater than himself, One who would eventually baptize the entire world with the Holy Spirit.

Occasionally, hecklers and wicked men came to make fun of John. He always knew when they were present, and, raising his voice, he would cry:

"Repent, you generation of vipers!"

129

At other times, wealthy persons, soldiers, and curiosity seekers, eager to see this strange prophet of God, would come and watch the baptisms take place. To these, John would say:

"If you are rich and wish to be saved, then share your wealth with the less fortunate. If you are a soldier and wish to be saved, then cease harming your fellow men."

A few faithful followers would then rise up and acclaim their leader as the Messiah and the Saviour of the world. But John would insist that he was only the forerunner of One mightier than he.

One day, as John was baptizing some of his followers, Jesus, now about thirty years old, came from Galilee to the River Jordan. Though Jesus and John were cousins, they had met only as children, for John spent most of his life in the desert. Nevertheless, the prophet recognized Jesus at once. Falling on his knees, he exclaimed:

"Behold! This is the One greater than I who will cleanse the world of its sins!"

Everyone was amazed. But Jesus said nothing. He advanced to the shore of the river and asked John to baptize him.

"You need not be baptized," said John. "You are the Son of God."

Jesus insisted, for he wished to know the experiences of all other men. So John baptized Jesus with the waters of the Jordan; and, as he did so, the clouds in the sky drew apart, a great burst of sunlight filled the scene, and, high above, a voice from Heaven could be heard proclaiming:

"This is My beloved Son, in whom I am well pleased."

Christ Baptized
in the Jordan
Drawing

10.

THE TEMPTATION OF JESUS

NOW, MORE THAN EVER, the Holy Spirit filled Jesus, and he realized his mission in life. In order to prepare and purify his soul, he went into seclusion for forty days, deep within the barren wilderness of Judea.

While Jesus was fasting and at his prayers, Satan, the devil, came up from the lower depths to tempt and torture him.

"You think you are the Son of God," Satan said. "Then prove it to me. Turn these stones into loaves of bread and ease your hunger."

But Jesus remained at his prayers and quietly said:

"My prayers are more important to me, for man shall not live by bread alone."

The devil laughed.

"Well then," he said. "If you are really the Son of God, throw yourself off the highest steeple of the Temple, and we will see if you are saved."

Jesus remained at his prayers and simply said:

"It is wrong to test God's powers by such a reckless act."

The devil was becoming impatient. Intent upon trapping Jesus and ruining his soul, he devised another plan.

"Worship me!" he pleaded, "and I will make you master over all the cities of the world, and over all the wealth within those cities."

Then, through his magic trickery, Satan caused an image of all the glittering cities of the world to appear in the barren desert.

Jesus did not hesitate a minute. Sternly, he exclaimed,

"Away, Satan, away! God and only God will I serve!"

With these strong words, the devil was cast down to the lower depths whence he had come. Then the angels of God descended and brought food and comfort to Jesus, who had proved, beyond all doubt, his purity and his love of God.

When he was refreshed, Jesus prepared to return to the River Jordan to find his cousin John. But then he heard some sorry news. The

Satan Showing Christ
the Kingdoms of the World
Drawing

new king Herod had arrested John for preaching against the sins of Herod's wicked wife. John was now in prison, perhaps being readied to die.

Jesus knew that it was best for him to return to Galilee and begin his ministry. He went to Capernaum near Nazareth. There he preached in the synagogue to the poor of the town.

"Repent!" he announced, "for the Kingdom of Heaven is at hand!"

11.

JESUS AND HIS FOLLOWERS

AFTER THE ARREST of John the Baptist, many of John's followers went into hiding. They were alone, now that their leader had gone. But some of the men remembered Jesus of Galilee, and recalled that John had said:

"This is the One greater than I."

John had also referred to Jesus as the "Lamb of God," which meant that Jesus would take upon himself the sins and sufferings of the world, like a lamb sacrificed upon the altar.

The followers of John who remembered these things were now prepared to follow Jesus.

Two of these men, Andrew and Simon, were brothers who earned their living as fishermen on the Sea of Galilee. One day, as Jesus was walking by the shores and meditating, he saw these brothers casting their nets into the waters.

Andrew recognized Jesus and was eager to follow him, but Simon was more reserved. As they were talking, a group of men and women came to the shore to hear Jesus preach. Often, persons met in out-of-the-

Christ Calls the Apostles
Simon and Andrew
Drawing

way places to listen to this young man of Nazareth, who seemed so filled with authority and holiness.

That day, the crowd was very large. Jesus turned to Simon and asked him if he might stand in the fishing boat, so that everyone could see him and hear better. Simon agreed.

After the sermon, when the crowd had dispersed, Jesus advised Simon to row out a bit farther and lower his nets. There he would find many fish, which Simon needed, for he had not been lucky in his catch that day. Simon followed this advice. To his amazement, he caught so many fish that his net was full and his boat so heavy that it almost sank. The following day, when he saw Jesus, Simon threw himself on the ground and cried:

"I am a sinful man because I hesitated to follow you. Now I know that you are the one for whom we have all been waiting, and I wish to do your bidding."

Jesus helped Simon to his feet and told him to come with him and with Andrew and the others who were eager to find salvation.

"I will make you fishers of men," he said.

Now the word spread that the teacher Jesus of Nazareth was calling the faithful to abandon their old lives and follow him to bring the message of God to the world. John and James, the two sons of a man named Zebedee, joined the group, to be followed by Philip and a man named Nathanael. In time, they were all to be known as the disciples, or those who teach. Tirelessly, they toured the cities of Galilee with Jesus, spreading the word of God.

The Miraculous
Draught of Fishes
Drawing

12.

THE WEDDING AT CANA

IN THE SMALL TOWN of Cana, there was to be a wedding. Among the honored guests were Jesus, his mother, and several of the disciples. In those days, a wedding feast took many days, and much food and wine was consumed.

Jesus only attended briefly, for he was busy preaching. He arrived toward the end of the feast, when all the wine had been drunk. Mary was a close friend of the host. She knew that he was greatly embarrassed to have no more wine, since an important official from the city was coming to pay his respects.

So Mary turned to her son, Jesus, and said:

"I know that you possess great powers. Can you help these friends? They have no wine and they expect an important guest."

Jesus had not yet performed any of the miracles that lay in his power. He did not wish to attract a following of those who would be impressed only with magic and sorcery, for his message appealed to the soul. Nevertheless, out of respect for his mother, Jesus decided to help the host. He told the servants to fetch six large pitchers used for water.

"Fill them with water from the well," he said.

The servants obeyed. Jesus had them carry the pitchers to the table. By this time, the high official of the city had arrived and was asking for a glass of wine.

The guests knew that there was no wine, and were amused when the servants brought the water pitchers to the table. But, to their amazement, when the colorless water was poured it turned into clear red wine. Everyone filled his cup and drank.

"Wonderful!" said the high official. "This is the finest wine I have ever tasted."

All the guests agreed, and complimented the host for saving the best wine until last. But the disciples of Jesus knew that a real miracle had occurred, and their faith and reverence for their master increased.

13.

JESUS PREACHES AND HEALS THE SICK

NOW THAT HE HAD changed the water to wine, Jesus was becoming famous in the area of Nazareth. He journeyed with his disciples to Capernaum again, and there he preached in the synagogue. It was the custom for learned men to give sermons and read lessons on the holidays.

While Jesus was preaching, a man in the congregation started to shout and call out insults and blasphemies. This man was unhappy and ill, but the people of the village simply thought he was insane and paid him no mind. Jesus came down from the pulpit, where he was preaching, and gently placed his hand on the angry man's shoulders. Then he lifted his eyes to God, and, soon, the man who had been shouting, his face red with rage, became quiet and calm. Everyone was deeply impressed, and the word spread fast that Jesus had the power to heal the sick with prayer.

Simon the fisherman, who had joined the disciples, was in need of Jesus' help. His mother-in-law lay ill with a serious fever and no doctor could relieve her. Jesus entered the house and straightway cured the elderly woman. All the curious neighbors who had crowded into the house were overwhelmed with astonishment. But Jesus wanted no praise. He left the cured woman and went to a solitary place to pray. There Simon followed him and declared himself a faithful disciple forevermore. With Jesus, he journeyed through Galilee preaching in the synagogues.

But it is always true that a famous man gathers enemies as well as friends. Many men of power became jealous and angry at the news that Jesus of Nazareth could heal the sick and cause great multitudes to follow him and accept his ideas.

One day, Jesus was preaching in the streets, when he heard a commotion nearby. The people were hurrying away in all directions because a leper was coming. A leper is afflicted with a terrible disease that causes flaking and scabbing of the skin. In those days it was thought that this disease was very contagious, and lepers were not allowed to mingle with other people. But this poor man wanted to be cured, and he dared venture into the streets to find Jesus.

"Make me clean again," the leper pleaded, "for no one will help me, and my life is meaningless."

Christ Healing
a Leper
Drawing

Christ Healing
a Leper
Drawing

In his great compassion, Jesus stretched forth his hands and touched the leper on the head. In that instant the horrible disease miraculously disappeared. Now, more than ever, the people praised Jesus—but his enemies also hated him all the more.

Time after time, in many ways and in many places, Jesus stretched forth his hand and cured the lame, the blind, and the suffering. He became so popular, in spite of his wish, that people lined up for hours to gain admittance to the house or the street where he was preaching.

One day, he was visiting a small house in Galilee. Such a great crowd had gathered that no one could get in or out of the door. Outside some people had brought a sick man on his bed so that Jesus might cure him. Because they could not force their way in through the door, they decided to remove the roof and lower the invalid down, bed and all. Some of Jesus' enemies were watching. They were always prepared to make fun of Jesus or to cast doubts upon his wisdom and holiness. Now, when they saw the sick man being lowered on his bed, they laughed aloud.

But Jesus admired the resourcefulness of the invalid and his friends, and he blessed them and stretched forth his hands. The man who, for years, had been unable to rise from his bed, now walked and was cured. He was so well, in fact, that he lifted the bed on his back and marched out of the house, praising God.

Jesus' enemies were angry. What right did this carpenter's son have to take upon himself the powers of God and the ancient prophets? they asked. Deliberately, they started to spread the word that Jesus was actually a sinner, a man who purposely broke the laws of God. This was like saying that night was day and black was white. But many aristocrats thought that Jesus was becoming too powerful and too well loved by the poor and unhappy people of Judea.

14.

THE CALLING OF MATTHEW

JESUS WAS always looking for upright men who could help him spread the word of God. He had felt that Simon, the fisherman, was such a man. Now he saw Matthew, and he wished him to join the great cause.

But Matthew was not a fisherman or a farmer. He pursued a very unpopular profession, and it caused him to be disliked and hated, for Matthew was a tax collector. It was his duty, though a Jew himself, to round up money from the Jews so that it might be paid to Herod and to Rome. Matthew was not happy in his work, but he knew that someone had to do it. Being kind by nature, he was, at least, a pleasant tax collector, and never persecuted anyone.

It was Jesus' hope that he would attract a following of many different kind of people; rich and poor, wise and simple, tax collectors as well as fishermen. One day, he approached the place where Matthew was counting taxes. Standing to the side, Jesus raised his arm and beckoned Matthew, saying:

"Follow me."

Matthew had heard of Jesus and believed in him. Without hesitation, he left his counting table, became one of the disciples, and, eventually, one of the authors of the Gospels.

Jesus' enemies were delighted with this latest piece of news. Imagine, they thought, now he has taken tax collectors into his company. Following Jesus to an inn, they confronted him and said:

"If you are a holy person sent by God, how can you sit here eating supper with tax collectors, beggars, and all sorts of common people?"

Jesus was never flustered by the question of his enemies. He smiled peacefully, and said:

"God has sent me to be a doctor to the sick. Why should I spend my time with those who are already well and sound? I must help the unhappy man, the hopeless man, and the sinner, whatever his calling or his station in life."

Thus Jesus spoke words and ideas that were new to the world, and, wherever he went, he gathered the sinners and the lowly, so that he might redeem them. But his detractors still complained.

"Why should God be concerned with sinners?" they asked.

And Jesus replied:

"God waits for all men to pay their debts to Him. The greater the debt, the greater the repentance, and the greater God's forgiveness."

To the fair-minded people of Judea, these words made sense. But the enemies of Jesus continued to argue and complain. When they heard that Jesus and his disciples had picked some grain to eat on the Sabbath day, they jumped on this infraction of the law, and cried out that Jesus had sinned. But the man from Nazareth simply reminded them that King David of old had done the same thing when he was hungry. David, in fact, had eaten the showbread meant for the rituals, yet the Lord did not punish him.

"That is all very well and good," said the enemies, "but you profane the Sabbath. You walk around preaching and do not go to the Temple."

Jesus answered quietly:

"A man need not be in the Temple to feel the presence of God, nor was man made just to worship on the Sabbath. The Sabbath was made for man."

Jesus' enemies even criticized him for curing the sick and suffering on the Sabbath. But Jesus explained:

"If you had a sheep and it fell into a pit on the Sabbath, you would not leave it there until the next day; by then it might be dead. Should we treat a sheep any better than we treat a man? No, God does not wish man to suffer needlessly, even on the Sabbath."

The enemies could not answer and turned away.

"This man Jesus must be destroyed," they whispered to themselves.

15.

JESUS VISITS JERUSALEM

AT DIFFERENT TIMES in his life, Jesus visited the great city of Jerusalem in order to worship at the Temple. The favorite time for such a visit was at Passover, the great celebration of the Jewish Exodus from Egypt under Moses.

With several of his disciples, Jesus came into Jerusalem unnoticed in the great throng of holiday visitors. At another time, in the not-too-distant future, he was to enter the city again, triumphantly—and he was to die there as well. This Jesus knew in his heart, but he said nothing to his disciples.

There was a man in Jerusalem to whom Jesus confided some of the most important concepts of his faith and of his mission on earth. This man was Nicodemus, a wealthy and influential Jew. One night, Nicodemus secretly sought out Jesus in a quiet room.

"I have heard of your miracles," said Nicodemus, "and I have listened to you speak. I want to know more about what you believe."

For many hours Jesus talked to Nicodemus. He told him that man was capable of everlasting life in the Kingdom of God, that, to enter this Kingdom, man had to have a pure heart and faith in God. Then Jesus reminded Nicodemus of the time when Moses fashioned a snake out of brass, so that people touching it might be saved from the poisonous bites of real serpents. Such a miracle would take place again through the Son of God, who, like the brazen snake, would be suspended on a cross and

Christ and Nicodemus
Drawing

die for the salvation of mankind. Jesus then revealed an amazing thing to Nicodemus.

"God so loved the world," he said, "that He gave His only begotten son, so that whoever believes in Him will not die, but will live forever."

Jesus did not say directly that he was the Son of God to Nicodemus —but, clearly, he was speaking of himself and envisioning the time of his own death and resurrection.

The visit with Nicodemus, including the discussion held that night, is one of the most important and meaningful events in the whole story of Jesus and his teachings.

16.

THE WOMAN AT THE WELL

AFTER THE PASSOVER FEAST, Jesus journeyed back to Galilee. He took the long way home, and thus passed through the land of Samaria, a place not friendly to the Jews. Jesus had a purpose in doing this, for he wanted to spread the word of God to people other than the Jews. So he went to the well in the center of the town of Sychar and sat there to rest. Soon a Samaritan woman came along to fetch some water.

"Would you give me a drink of water?" Jesus asked. The woman was surprised. Usually, Jews did not speak to Samaritans, let alone ask them for water.

"Why do you ask me?" she said.

"If you knew who I am," he answered, "you would ask me to give *you* the living waters that I possess."

The woman was confused. She wanted to know what waters he meant. Jesus said:

"Whoever drinks of ordinary water soon becomes thirsty again. But if you drink the waters I bring, you will never be thirsty again and you will have everlasting life."

The Samaritan woman became all excited. Naturally, she wanted

Christ and
the Samaritan Woman
Oil on panel

some of this wonderful water, and asked Jesus to provide it. She did not understand that he was not speaking of real water, but of faith.

"First, you must purify your heart," said Jesus to the woman, "for I know that you are a sinner and have done some wicked things."

The woman blushed. It was true, she had been wicked. Realizing that she was talking to a religious prophet, the woman tried to excuse herself by saying:

"I am not a Jew, and I do not worship as you do."

Jesus assured her that the message and blessings of God were meant for all mankind, and that God had chosen the Jews as a means of bringing this salvation to the world.

"I know," the woman said. "I have heard that the Messiah called Christ will come from them—and that the whole world awaits him."

Jesus then spoke some startling words.

"I am he, the Messiah," he said.

The Samaritan woman was thus the first one to hear, directly from Jesus' own lips, these magnificent words. She immediately believed what she heard and rushed off to spread the news.

Jesus remained at the well. Soon some of his disciples came along with food, which they had purchased in the city.

But Jesus did not eat. His talk with the Samaritan woman had so filled his spirit that he felt no need of food. Later, he preached in Samaria at the well where he had revealed his divinity to the humble Samaritan woman.

17.

THE SERMON ON THE MOUNT

ALL OVER GALILEE, in Syria, to the north and to the south, the word of Jesus' powers and holiness was spreading. Multitudes of people came to hear the Master and to be cured by his outstretched hand. Though Jesus knew that this was his role on earth, he nevertheless shunned the praises and adulation of the crowds. Often, he would stand

Jesus and
His Disciples
Drawing

in a small boat at the water's edge while the people listened from the shore. Then he would preach and heal, and, straightway, he would leave the scene to meditate by himself in the hills.

To assist in his great work, Jesus appointed twelve of his followers to be apostles, and thus to possess the powers of healing and the insight to preach the Word of God. These apostles were Simon the fisherman, who was later called Peter; Andrew, his brother; James and John the sons of Zebedee; Philip; Bartholomew; Thomas; Matthew the tax collector; James Alpheus; Thaddeus; Simon from Canaan; and a man named Judas Iscariot. These twelve preached to the people, as Jesus had instructed them.

Then one day, as he was meditating, Jesus saw thousands of people wending their way up the side of the mountain so that they might hear him preach. He called his disciples and told them to prepare the throng, for he would make a sermon there on the mountain, and, in this sermon, he would say all those things that mankind had to know for its salvation. The undying words he spoke that day are beyond compare in all history. He said:

> Blessed are the poor in spirit:
> for theirs is the kingdom of heaven.
> Blessed are they that mourn:
> for they shall be comforted.
> Blessed are the meek:
> for they shall inherit the earth.

Blessed are they which do hunger and
 thirst after righteousness:
 for they shall be filled.
Blessed are the merciful:
 for they shall obtain mercy.
Blessed are the pure in heart:
 for they shall see God.
Blessed are the peacemakers:
 for they shall be called the
 children of God.
Blessed are they which are persecuted
 for righteousness' sake:
 for theirs is the kingdom of heaven.
Blessed are ye, when men shall revile you,
 and persecute you,
 and shall say all manner of evil against you
 falsely, for my sake.
Rejoice and be exceeding glad: for great is
 your reward in heaven:
 for so persecuted they the prophets
 which were before you.

The blessings that Jesus pronounced are called the Beatitudes. They were the first part of his Sermon on the Mount. In the second part, Jesus went on to assure the Jews that his task was not to upset the Laws of Moses, but, rather, to fulfill them. For that reason he recited the famous Golden Rule: *Do unto others as you would have them do unto you.*

He also gave the humble and the poor great hope and courage, for he told them that they did not need wealth and high station to enter the Kingdom of God, but, rather, righteousness and purity. Recalling the Ten Commandments, he warned that if we hate a man without cause and wish him dead, it is as if we murder him. He then urged the people to be merciful and forgiving, even with their enemies, and he said:

"Whosoever shall smite thee on thy right cheek, turn to him the other, also."

By this he meant: do not hastily strike back at someone who attacks you, but, rather, show him the peaceful intentions of your heart.

Furthermore, Jesus inspired the people to believe that God was always with them. They did not need the Temple, he said, or the synagogue, or the elaborate rituals of their religion to feel the presence of God and to become holy. Instead of repetitious prayers and chantings, Jesus taught a simple prayer, which all men might offer, for he said:

"Your Father in Heaven knows what is in your hearts."

The words he pronounced are called the Lord's Prayer, the most beautiful prayer in all the world:

> Our Father which art in heaven,
> Hallowed be thy name.
> Thy kingdom come.
> Thy will be done in earth,
>   as it is in heaven.
> Give us this day our daily bread.
> And forgive us our debts,
>   as we forgive our debtors.
> And lead us not into temptation,
>   but deliver us from evil:
> For Thine is the kingdom, and the power,
>   and the glory, for ever. Amen.

After this, Jesus spoke many more immortal words, and taught the meaning of faith and love, of justice, and salvation. Then he departed, and left the people astonished and inspired beyond all their dreams.

18.

JESUS SAVES TWO YOUNG MEN

IN THE CITY of Capernaum there were about one hundred Roman soldiers stationed to keep the peace. At the head of this small army was a centurion, or a captain, as we would call him. He lived very well and

The Centurion
Kneeling Before Christ
Drawing

had many servants, one of whom became quite ill. The centurion loved this servant like a son, and was distressed to see him suffering without hope of being cured.

Jesus was in Capernaum, and the centurion sent word beseeching him to save his dying servant. The disciples told Jesus that this Roman had been very kind to the Jews, and that he had even helped them build their synagogue. Jesus went to the centurion's house immediately. But as he approached, the centurion's messengers came running down the stairs with a note from their master. It said:

"Lord, I do not feel worthy enough to have you honor my house, nor do I think myself worthy to appear in person before you. But I have great faith that you can cure my servant without seeing him, even as I command many soldiers whom I do not know. I beg you to show mercy."

Jesus was deeply impressed with such faith. Moreover, he rejoiced to see that people other than the Jews were accepting his teachings and his power. He prayed for the dying man. That night, the centurion found that a miracle had taken place, and that his servant was well.

In the city of Nain, a poor widow was in grief. Her only son, her hope and support, had died of a fever. Jesus came to see the widow and found her kneeling beside the bed on which her son's body was laid. With great compassion, Jesus stretched forth his hand and called out:

"Young man, arise and live."

To everyone's amazement the boy who had been dead arose as one awakes in the morning, and embraced his mother. Soon the entire country heard about this miracle, and many, many more people began to believe that Jesus of Nazareth was indeed the Saviour of whom the prophets had spoken.

Yet many also doubted and hated Jesus. Some were sincere, others merely wicked. The followers of John the Baptist were honest in their doubts of Jesus, for they believed John to be the Messiah. After all, they said, John lived a life of pain and suffering in the desert; he never ate meat or drank wine; he now awaits death in Herod's prison. Is he not the real Messiah?

Jesus understood their doubts.

"You can't imagine that the Saviour should come to you neatly dressed, eating with tax collectors, going to weddings, and drinking wine. But God is wise, and knows what He is doing."

Then he continued:

"Come unto me, all you that labor and are heavy laden and I will give you rest."

19.

THE REJECTION IN NAZARETH
AND THE SINFUL WOMAN

JESUS WAS ESPECIALLY anxious to preach in Nazareth, where he had spent most of his life. There his mother Mary lived and his father, Joseph the carpenter, was buried. One day, Jesus asked permission to preach in the synagogue at Nazareth, and, according to custom, he was invited to do so.

Taking the Book of the Law in his hand, Jesus read about his own ministry among the poor and suffering, just as the prophets had described it many hundreds of years before. Though Jesus was very convincing in his speech, the elders of the synagogue in Nazareth rejected him.

"Isn't this the carpenter's son?" they asked in ridicule. "Is he trying

The Woman Taken
in Adultery
Drawing

The Woman Taken
in Adultery
Oil on panel

to say that he is the Messiah of whom the prophets wrote?" And they laughed.

Jesus' disciples were unhappy to see their master rejected, especially in his own home town. But Jesus was philosophical.

"No prophet is accepted in his own country," he said. "Therefore, we must preach among other people. After all, you remember how Elisha, the prophet, converted Naaman, a man from Syria. God wishes us to spread His word among all the people of the world."

So they went on their way, preaching and teaching in the nearby towns. As usual, the enemies of Jesus followed close behind. They hoped to trap Jesus in public, so that the people would no longer believe in him. For this purpose, they brought a sinful woman into his presence. This woman had been unfaithful to her husband—a crime punishable by stoning, according to the ancient laws.

"What would you do with this wicked woman?" shouted Jesus' enemies. Jesus was silent at first. He stooped down and wrote something in the sand at his feet.

The enemies smiled. They thought they had truly trapped Jesus. If he said that the sinful woman should go free, they could accuse him of disobeying the sacred laws. And if he condemned the woman and had her stoned to death, they could say that he was cruel and without mercy.

Jesus sought neither path. He rose and said simply:

"He that is without sin among you, let him cast the first stone at her."

Everyone was amazed. For in that crowd there was no one without sin—and no one worthy of condemning another human being. One by one, the conscience-stricken people left the scene until Jesus was alone with the sinful woman.

147

"We must not condemn each other," said Jesus to the woman. "We must forgive and pray to be forgiven. Go then, and sin no more."

The sinful woman was so grateful to Jesus that she became one of his followers. Some believe that this was Mary of Magdala, or Mary Magdalene. It is also said that, one night, while Jesus was dining in a rich man's house, Mary Magdalene entered with rare spices and oil so that she might anoint Jesus' feet. In those days, people always removed their shoes when they went inside, and bathed their feet and sprinkled them with fine spices and oils.

Magdalene anointed Jesus' feet with her tears and dried them with her long blonde hair. Then she sprinkled them with spices and oil. The rich man at whose table Jesus was dining watched all this in surprise, and wondered how Jesus could allow a woman of such bad reputation to touch him, let alone anoint his feet.

Jesus spoke softly and reminded his host that God forgives all sinners who repent; the greater the sin, the greater is the repentance and the greater God's forgiveness.

"You are a rich man," said Jesus to his host. "But when I came into your house tonight, you did not anoint my feet and sprinkle them with spices and oil. You think your sins are few and you need not repent. But this woman knows her sins, and they are great. Thus will she be forgiven."

Then Jesus told a parable, to illustrate his point. Two men owed money to another man. One owed five hundred pieces of silver, the other only fifty. The man to whom the money was owed was generous and disclaimed both debts. Which of the debtors do you think was most appreciative? asked Jesus. And the rich host answered:

"The man who owed five hundred pieces of silver."

"Exactly," Jesus replied. "He who is forgiven the most will love the most. Just as this woman whom I forgave loves me and believes in me more than you do."

Christ Preaching
Before the Pharisees
Drawing

20.

JESUS ANSWERS HIS ENEMIES

NO MATTER HOW KINDLY Jesus spoke and how wisely he proved his teachings, his enemies taunted him and tried to cast doubts upon his mission. They began to spread the rumor that Jesus was in league with the devil himself, because he cured people and brought them back from death. They argued that, since the devil brought about disease and suffering, only the devil could call them off.

Jesus answered boldly:

"How can Satan cast out Satan?" he asked. "If a house is divided against itself, that house cannot stand. The fact is that God and only God can undo the devil's treachery, and you who are evil at heart cannot know good or speak wisely."

Then Jesus spoke of Jonah, who had been three days in the belly of a whale.

"So shall the Son of Man be three days in the heart of the earth," said Jesus. But no one grasped the meaning of these prophetic words.

In the crowd listening to Jesus were Mary, his mother, and his brothers and sisters. When someone pointed them out to him, Jesus exclaimed:

"All people are my brothers and sisters, for all of us have the same Father, who is God in heaven."

21.

PARABLES OF THE SOWER
AND OF THE KINGDOM OF GOD

JESUS WAS A GREAT TEACHER because he made his lessons clear and easily understandable. To do this, he often told parables, or stories with a message. One day, while standing in a boat on the shores of Galilee, Jesus told this story to the crowd:

A farmer filled his apron with seeds, and set off to scatter them in the fresh earth. As he tossed the seeds this way and that way, some fell by the wayside, where the blackbirds ate them; some fell upon stony places; some fell among the brambles; and others fell into the earth, as they were supposed to. Jesus explained the story to his disciples.

"My words are like the seeds," he said. "Some will fall by the wayside and be ignored, so that the devil, like a blackbird, will come and eat them up. Some will fall upon people who are like rocks where no seed can take root, and therefore perishes. My words will also fall among brambles—among people who are too caught up with other things, such as money and pleasure, to concern themselves with the teachings of God. And my words will also fall upon those people, who, like fresh earth, are ready and willing to accept them and let them grow and bear fruit. This is the meaning of my parable."

Jesus often used the example of seeds being scattered in the fields as a way of clarifying his message. He knew that many of the people who listened to him were farmers and would understand the comparisons. Once, he compared heaven to a mustard seed, which is the least imposing of all seeds until it grows. Then it becomes a great tree, with many branches upon which many birds may live.

22.

THE GREAT STORM AT SEA

AFTER TELLING his parables, Jesus decided it was time to travel, and he beckoned his disciples to follow him across the Sea of Galilee to the distant shore. They all boarded a ship, which then set sail.

Jesus was weary. He stretched out on the deck and soon fell fast asleep. As the ship made its way across the sea, a ferocious storm began brewing in the heavens. Within minutes, thunder and lightning were striking, and great waves were tossing the ship without mercy.

The disciples became fearful of their lives. Rushing to Jesus, they roused him from his sleep, crying:

"Save us, Master, save us!"

Without hesitation, Jesus lifted his arms and ordered the heavens to be at peace. In that same instant, the storm subsided and the great waves disappeared, so that the sea was peaceful and calm. Then Jesus turned to his friends and said:

"Why did you doubt that you would be saved? If I am with you, and you believe in me, then you will never perish."

The disciples, who knew Jesus and had seen his miracles before, were nonetheless amazed that he could command the very heavens themselves to obey.

When the ship docked on the far side of the sea, Jesus beheld a poor, sick man wandering in the graveyards of the countryside. This man, long afflicted with madness, had been abandoned by his family and friends. Now he was alone and he could do nothing but cause himself harm.

Jesus approached this piteous person and asked his name.

The man replied:

"My name is Legion."

By this, he meant that there were many sorry souls like him throughout the world possessed by many demons. Jesus lifted his hands and ordered the evil spirits out of the man and into the bodies of some swine that were feeding nearby. Then these swine ran, possessed, into the sea and disappeared.

The Storm on
the Sea of Galilee
Oil on canvas

151

Now the man whose name was Legion was cured, and he begged to join the disciples. But Jesus urged him to stay among his own people and spread the word of God, for the people would believe him, seeing him cured and having known how hopeless he once had been.

23.

JAIRUS' DAUGHTER

JESUS AND THE DISCIPLES returned to Capernaum aboard their ship. This time the sea was calm. But upon the shore a great crowd awaited with excitement, for many had come to be healed.

Most eager in the crowd was Jairus, a high official of the synagogue. His twelve-year-old daughter lay dying, and he knew that only Jesus could save her. As the Master set foot on the shore, Jairus rushed forward and begged Jesus to hasten to his house and save his child. Jesus immediately responded and started to make his way through the crowd.

Waiting on a side road was an elderly woman who had suffered from a blood disease for many years. Countless doctors had been unable to help her; now she knew that Jesus was her only hope. But, as he passed, the crowd was so thick that she could not speak to him. Hurriedly she followed behind, having faith that to touch the hem of his robe would be enough to cure her illness. With great effort, the elderly woman managed to place her fingers just at the hem of the Master's robe.

Though hundreds of people pressed in from every side, Jesus knew that someone in need of him had touched his robe. He stopped and turned.

"Who touched me?" he inquired.

Christ and the
Ailing Woman
Drawing

"Everyone is touching you," his disciples replied, "for the crowd is very large."

"Yes," said Jesus, "but there is someone here who was ill and now she is healed, for I felt my curative powers entering her soul."

The sickly woman fearfully raised her hand and admitted that she had touched the Master. Jesus was pleased.

"So great is this woman's faith," he said, "that she need but touch my robe to be healed."

At this same moment a messenger came running toward Jairus with the terrible news that his daughter had died. The poor man broke down in tears. But Jesus spoke words of comfort.

"Only believe," he said, "and all will be well."

Then Jesus hastened to Jairus' house, where many people were mourning and weeping.

"She is dead," they said to Jesus. "Why try to save her now?"

"She is not dead," Jesus replied. "She is merely asleep."

Though the others were scornful, he went to the little girl's bed and commanded her to rise. Miraculously, the child opened her eyes and walked from her bed into the arms of her joyous parents.

"Give her something to eat," said Jesus, "and tell no one of this miracle. I do not perform these deeds in order to win praise, but to prove the power of God."

After this, Jesus journeyed through the streets, and blind men and deaf mutes followed him and cried out their faith in his powers, so that they were cured. From Capernaum to the shores of Galilee, in the cities beyond, the word spread fast; no one had ever seen such miracles as the miracles of Jesus.

The Raising of
the Daughter of Jairus
Drawing

24.

THE DISCIPLES ARE INSTRUCTED
AND MANY PERSONS ARE FED

TIME WAS SHORT and Jesus had a great deal of work to do. In order to spread the word of God, he instructed his twelve disciples in the purposes of his mission and he endowed them with the miraculous power of healing.

"Heal the sick, cleanse the lepers, raise the dead, cast out devils," he said, "and ask nothing in return."

He further warned them to be very careful.

"I send you forth as sheep in the midst of wolves," he said. "Therefore, be as wise as serpents and as harmless as doves."

The disciples were inspired, and set off for many distant cities in order to heal and preach in the manner of Jesus.

Weeks later, the disciples joined Jesus again. They saw how hard he had worked and urged him to rest. But, as he went up to a quiet place in order to sit beneath a shade tree, he found a great throng of people awaiting him.

"They are like sheep without a shepherd," said Jesus, and, forgetting his own need of rest, he went into the midst of the crowd and preached.

By evening, more people had joined the throng, and all were hungry. The disciples thought that it was time to send them home to eat.

"No," said Jesus. "They are poor and we must feed them."

"But we have only a few pennies," answered the disciples, "not enough for even a small loaf of bread."

Jesus looked around. Seated nearby was a boy with a picnic basket. In the basket were five loaves of bread and two small fish. Jesus took the food and performed a great miracle. With only five loaves of bread and two little fish, he was able to feed five thousand people, and, when they were done eating, there were twelve baskets of food left over.

The throng was astonished. They wanted to make Jesus king and put him on a throne. But Jesus wished no such earthly praise, and he quietly left the scene and disappeared into the hills.

25.

JESUS WALKS ON THE WATER

AFTER THE MIRACLE of the loaves and fishes, Jesus instructed his disciples to cross the Sea of Galilee, so that they might continue their preaching. He stood on the shore bidding them good-by as they set sail.

However, when night fell, the sea became very rough, and the disciples had a hard time rowing the boat. Suddenly, they saw a figure apparently walking on the water. At first, they were afraid, because it was dark and they could not recognize their Master. But, once Jesus made himself known, they rejoiced.

Peter had doubted that anyone could walk on the sea, and asked Jesus to endow him with the same power. Stepping out of the boat at Jesus' bidding, Peter found that he could also walk upon the waves. But, suddenly, a wind blew up and Peter became afraid, thus losing faith. Immediately, he began to sink. Jesus rescued him, saying:

"Man of little faith, why did you doubt?"

Peter was ashamed, but now, more than ever, he was convinced of his Master's divinity. Later, Jesus sat among his disciples and asked them:

"Who do you think I really am?"

Some said that he was the prophet Jeremiah, reborn, or Isaiah, or even Elijah. But Peter said:

Christ Walking
on Water
Drawing

"You are Christ, the Son of the Living God."

Jesus was deeply impressed with Peter's understanding and faith, and he said to him:

"You, Peter, are the rock upon which I will build my church, and you will also sit at the gates of heaven and hold the keys to my kingdom in your hands."

The other disciples now realized that their Master was indeed the Messiah, the Christ, for whom the world had prayed. But Jesus warned them not to speak of this news in public.

26.

THE MISSION OF MERCY CONTINUES

FOR MANY MONTHS, Jesus and his disciples traveled through Galilee and other parts of the Holy Land, curing the sick, preaching, and debating their ideas. Jesus made no distinction among the suffering. Jews and gentiles (or foreigners) were healed by him. Children and old people came to be comforted; the blind and deaf, the sick in body and mind, all were saved by faith in his word and teachings.

But, still, the scribes and the Pharisees and the rulers of the cities believed Jesus to be a dangerous and troublesome man. In spite of the proofs of his power, these enemies of Jesus continued to plan ways to ensnare and perhaps destroy him.

Yet he continued his work. One day, at the city of Bethsaida, Jesus restored a blind man's sight. Later, he healed an epileptic boy.

Jesus also continued to instruct his disciples in the ways of the Lord. It was important that they be able to answer their enemies, so that the people would respect their wisdom.

Once a tax collector stopped Peter, and said to him:

"You are a follower of Jesus, and he says many things about the proper way to live; but, tell me, does he pay his taxes?"

Peter immediately answered, "Yes."

Nevertheless, Peter wondered if Jesus, a divine being from God, should actually have to pay taxes, for a king did not pay taxes in Judea. He asked Jesus about this, and Jesus replied:

"I will pay the tax and keep the peace. We want no trouble over such a little matter."

"Very well," said Peter, "but there is no money to pay the tax."

"Go to the sea," said Jesus, "and cast your line."

Peter did so. The first fish he caught had a coin in its mouth. Peter took the coin, sought out the tax collector and said:

"Here is my master's tax."

Thus, the disciples learned the proper conduct of their lives. But they learned the hard way.

One day, they were arguing among themselves about which one of them was the most important and would, thus, receive the most reward in Jesus' eyes. Jesus overheard this foolish argument, and he said:

"If any man desires to be first in the kingdom of heaven then he must really be last; he must be humble, serve others, do good things, and expect no reward. But he who thinks of himself as great and righteous and expects all others to honor him, he shall be considered lowly in the eyes of God."

Jesus then prophesied his own death and resurrection, and said that many would come after him who would take up the burden of his work and suffer the same fate, but that they who did so and died for the cause would gain eternal life in heaven.

"What does a man profit if he gains the whole world," said Jesus, "but gives up his chance to live after death?"

27.

THE TRANSFIGURATION

SOMETHING JESUS HAD SAID troubled the disciples, and they spoke of it among themselves.

"What did he mean about his death and resurrection?" they asked.

Several times now, Jesus had made reference to a time, not far off, when he would go to Jerusalem, be condemned, and later be forced to carry a weighty cross upon which he would die. Then, Jesus said, he would rise from the dead, after three days, to show all the world God's great mercy and power. The disciples could not understand the mystery and wonder of these prophecies.

Jesus did not explain further. One night, he asked three of his followers, Peter, John, and James, to walk with him to a high mountain in the north country. He wanted to pray there.

The three men walked with Jesus and became weary. When they reached the peak, they lay down, wrapped their cloaks about them, and slept. Jesus, meanwhile, knelt in prayer. Then a wonderful thing happened: the heavens opened, a great light poured forth, and two mighty figures appeared, as though on a golden staircase. They were Moses and Elijah, the great ancient prophets of God. They had come to speak with Jesus, the Messiah.

The bright light and the glory of this moment roused Peter and his friends from their sleep. When Peter saw the figures of Moses and Elijah and the transfiguration of Jesus into a being of radiance and great beauty, he fell on his knees and cried out:

"Let me build a temple here to commemorate this great moment." But, as he spoke, a voice was heard far above, saying:

"Behold, this is My beloved Son in whom I am well pleased. Believe in him, and that is enough."

When Peter raised his head, the vision had disappeared, leaving Jesus in a glowing light. Now, more than ever, Peter and his friends knew that their Master was the Son of God, in other words, God in the form of man. But Jesus advised them to keep this knowledge to themselves. Again, he foresaw his fate in Jerusalem, but he comforted his disciples, saying:

"Even my death is part of God's great plan."

28.

THE GOOD SAMARITAN

THE TEACHING of God's word was now going forth with great speed. Jesus appointed seventy righteous men to visit seventy cities in order to preach. Others took up the task of healing: and many evil spirits were cast out of the land.

Still Jesus' enemies tried to ensnare him. One day a lawyer stood up and called out to Jesus:

"How shall I achieve eternal life? What is the way?"

And Jesus answered:

"You shall love the Lord your God with all your heart, and you shall love your neighbor as yourself."

The lawyer was cunning, and he said:

"Love my neighbor? How do I know who my neighbor is? Suppose he is a stranger to me?"

To answer this insincere question, Jesus told a parable, as follows:

Once a certain man was journeying from Jerusalem to Jericho, when he was suddenly attacked by robbers, who left him badly beaten and stripped by the side of the road. As the poor man lay there, a high-and-mighty priest rode by. Seeing the suffering man, he turned his face and quickly galloped away. He wanted no part of any trouble. Similarly, a Levite, one of the officials of the Temple, came by, looked at the injured man, and also hurried off without trying to help.

Then a humble man from Samaria, a Samaritan as he was called, journeyed by and, seeing the wounded man, rushed to his aid, and care-

The Good Samaritan
at the Inn
Drawing

The Good Samaritan
at the Inn
Oil on canvas

The Good Samaritan
Drawing

fully dressed his injuries. Then the Samaritan lifted him onto his horse and took him to a nearby inn to recuperate. Moreover, when morning dawned, the Samaritan gave the unfortunate man some money, so that he might find his way home.

Now Jesus turned to the lawyer and asked:

"Which of the three men would you consider the neighbor of the injured man?"

And the lawyer answered:

"The Samaritan, because he helped him and showed him mercy."

"Indeed," said Jesus, "we are all neighbors if we show mercy to each other. Now you go and do the same."

29.

THE MAN BORN BLIND

A POOR BEGGAR lay in the streets, blind and helpless. Jesus was passing, and took pity on the man, who begged for comfort. Taking some clay from the ground, Jesus moistened it and applied it to the blind man's eyes. Then he told him to wash himself in the pool at Siloam, nearby.

The beggar obeyed, and, when he had finished bathing, he found his sight restored and his whole body well and straight. He returned to his home to declare the wondrous miracles of Jesus. But his neighbors

Christ Healing
a Blind Man
Drawing

were suspicious. They didn't believe that this healthy-looking man was the same beggar whom they had seen every day lying in the streets.

Jesus' enemies took advantage of the situation. They implied that the so-called blind man was a fraud. Some people sought out the beggar's parents and asked them, "Is this your son, and was he ever really blind?"

The old people realized they might get in trouble with the high priests and the rich men of the city so they simply replied:

"He is old enough to answer for himself."

The beggar was angry, and insisted that he had been blind since birth and that Jesus had miraculously restored his sight. But he was greeted with threats and ridicule. Discouraged, he sought out Jesus for comfort, recalling that Jesus had once said, "None is so blind as he who will not see."

30.

THE RAISING OF LAZARUS

IN THE TOWN of Bethany lived Lazarus and his two sisters, Martha and Mary. They believed in Jesus, and knew that he was the Messiah sent from God. Such knowledge made all three very happy.

But, now, sad times befell the family, for Lazarus was grievously ill, and his sisters feared that he would die. Hurriedly they sent word to Jesus, who was preaching nearby.

"Come and save our brother, your friend Lazarus," they pleaded.

But, oddly enough, Jesus did not seem anxious. Instead, he continued his mission, telling his disciples that Lazarus' illness was part of God's plan.

Then one day word came of Lazarus' death. Now Jesus was determined to go to Bethany. His disciples begged him to remain where he was. Once, in Bethany, some people had thrown stones at him, because they said he had broken the Sabbath. But Jesus was not afraid.

"Our friend Lazarus is asleep, and I must wake him," he said.

The disciples were confused. They thought Lazarus was dead, not asleep. Nevertheless, they followed their Master into Bethany.

It took Jesus four days to arrive at the home of Lazarus. It was a house of sorrow. Many people had gathered to comfort Martha and Mary, the grieving sisters. When Jesus appeared, Martha ran to him.

"Oh Lord," she said, "if only you had come sooner, you could have saved our brother. Now he lies in his grave these last four days."

Jesus spoke comforting words.

"Lazarus will rise again," he said.

"I know," Martha replied, "he will arise on Judgment Day, in the Resurrection, for he was a righteous man. But, for now, he is gone and buried."

Jesus then proclaimed a mighty message.

"I am the Resurrection and the Life," he said. "Whosoever believes in me, *though he be dead*, he shall live again. And whosoever lives and believes in me, he shall never die."

With these words ringing in her ears, Martha led Jesus to the tomb of Lazarus. Meanwhile Mary had heard of the Master's arrival. She rushed from the house in the midst of all the mourners, seemingly joyful, for she knew the power of the Lord.

At Lazarus' tomb, the sisters knelt and wept with Jesus, who had great compassion in his heart. All those around them were struck by Jesus' devotion, and wondered could he, who had cured the lame and the blind, also raise from the dead a man buried four days in the earth?

Jesus ordered the stone rolled away from the tomb of Lazarus. Then, lifting his eyes to heaven, he cried,

"Lazarus, come forth!"

The Raising
of Lazarus
Etching

The Raising
of Lazarus
Oil on panel

God heard Jesus' prayer, and, in a miracle surpassing all others, He restored Lazarus to life, so that the man who had been dead emerged from his tomb, still wrapped in his shroud, and stood before the astonished crowd.

Word of this mighty miracle reached the priests and rulers of Jerusalem. The most influential of these men was Caiaphas, a high priest of the Temple. He was very crafty and knew how to balance his power between the Jews and the Romans who ruled the nation.

"If this man Jesus becomes too powerful," he said, "the Romans will get angry and cause us harm. We must rid ourselves of this so-called Messiah from Galilee."

At first, it was thought to exile Jesus. But he would not leave his country or abandon his work, for the people now joined him in greater numbers. Some openly approached him in the streets and asked to become disciples.

"Do you know that it is hard to be a disciple of mine?" Jesus would inquire. Some agreed, but joined him. Others found the task too hard, and fell by the wayside. Jesus understood, for he was always aware of man's weaknesses. Once, he said: "Many are called, but few are chosen."

31.

SOME FAMOUS PARABLES

JESUS CONTINUED to preach his parables, using examples from everyday life. He told the story of *The Missing Coin.*

Once, he said, there was a woman who had ten silver coins. By accident, one of them rolled off the table to the floor. The woman was determined to find that coin, so she lit her candle and began searching in every corner of the room. When she found the missing piece, she was so overjoyed that she threw open the windows and called to her neighbors:

"Rejoice with me, for I have found the coin I lost."

In this same way, said Jesus, God rejoices when even one lost sinner repents.

Another story had the same message. It was the *Parable of the Prodigal Son*. Once there were two brothers who lived at home with their father. The younger was impatient and restless. He wanted to see the world and enjoy the life of the big cities outside. Accordingly, he asked his father to give him his share of his inheritance, so that he might venture forth into the world.

The father did as his youngest son asked; and the boy went off to the city. There he gambled and lived a riotous life, until he was without money and friends. Then a famine came upon the land. Poor, disgraced, and hopeless, the young man made his way back home. It was his plan to become a servant in his father's house, so that he might pay off his debts and make himself worthy once again.

As he approached the house, his father saw him and ran to greet him joyously.

"But, father," said the prodigal son, "I am not worthy of your forgiveness, for I have sinned."

The father would hear no more. He ordered the finest robes brought from the house, and arranged a splendid feast to be held in celebration of his son's return. The older brother became angry.

"I have been faithful and steadfast," he said to his father, "but with no reward. My brother, however, wasted your money and disgraced himself in the big cities. Now you throw a banquet to celebrate his return."

The father smiled.

"I do not love you less than your brother," he said, "but it is fitting that we should make merry and be glad; for your brother was as good as dead, but now he is alive again. He was lost, and now he is found."

Some of Jesus' parables concerned the Pharisees, who had set them-

The Departure of
the Prodigal Son
Drawing

The Prodigal Son
with Loose Women
Drawing

selves against all new ideas and prophecies. In one story called *The Beggar and the Pharisee,* a poor man named Lazarus, who was too ill to work, stationed himself at the door of a rich Pharisee's home. There he lay, hoping to catch a few crumbs from the rich man's table. But he was ignored, and chased by dogs in his misery. Finally Lazarus died and went to heaven, where the angels carried him to the comfort and peace of Abraham's bosom.

In time, the rich Pharisee also died. But he did not go to heaven. Instead he fell among flames and torture, so that he lay in perpetual agony. From this wretched place, the rich man could see Lazarus, the beggar, in Abraham's bosom, and he called to him and cried:

"Help me. I am thirsty and in pain. Just dip your finger in some water so that I may wet my lips."

But the gulf between Lazarus and the rich man was too great, and the beggar could not help him. The Pharisee, realizing the error of his ways, sought to prevent his brothers and his sons from knowing a similar fate. So he cried out to Lazarus:

"Go back to earth, and warn my kinsmen of the fate that awaits them if they remain hard-hearted and cruel."

But the angels said:

"Your kinsmen have the Bible and the law as a guide. What good is it to send Lazarus to them if they will not repent after reading the word of God?"

Jesus told a similar story of the *Pharisee and the Publican.* The publican was a humble man of modest station in Jerusalem. Compared to a mighty Pharisee, he was considered of little importance. Once a rich Pharisee and a humble publican went to the Temple to pray. The Pharisee raised his eyes toward Heaven and said:

"I am a righteous man, not like the others. I pray; I give money to the Temple; and I fast twice a week."

The publican standing nearby lowered his eyes and bowed his head. His prayer was quite different.

"I am a lowly sinner," he said, "and I can only pray for my forgiveness."

Jesus assured his listeners that God was much more impressed with the publican than with the Pharisee, for, as Jesus said, he who exalts

The Return of the
Prodigal Son
Oil on canvas

The Return of
the Prodigal Son
Etching

165

himself shall be brought low, and he who humbles himself shall be exalted in the eyes of God.

Jesus told another parable about wealth and humility:

A rich young Pharisee once came to Jesus and asked:

"How may I gain eternal life?"

Jesus reminded the young man of the law and the Commandments.

"Yes," said the Pharisee. "I have obeyed the law and I follow the Commandments, but I feel that there is something else I must do."

Jesus knew what the rich man lacked.

"Go," he said to him. "Sell all your possessions and give the money to the poor. Make yourself a disciple of mine, and you shall inherit a greater treasure in heaven."

But the rich man could not bring himself to part with his worldly goods, so he went away with his head hung low. Then Jesus turned to his friends and said:

"How hard it is for a wealthy man to part with his goods. Indeed, it is easier for a camel to pass through the eye of a needle than for a rich man to enter the Kingdom of God."

The people loved to hear Jesus' parables, for they were easily understood and dealt with everyday events. For example:

A man had four servants who were very trustworthy. Because he was going on a long journey, the man divided his money among the servants and told them to take good care of it. Three of the servants took the money and invested it so that they could show a profit when their master returned. But the fourth servant was lazy, and merely buried the money in the ground. Of course, money does not grow in the ground. So, when

The Parable of
the Talents
Drawing

The Parable of
the King Who Took
Account of His Servants
Drawing

The Parable of the
Laborers in the Vineyard
Drawing

Christ Conversing
with Martha and Mary
Drawing

the master returned, the clever servants were able to show a profit, but the lazy man could only hand back the same amount of money he had been given. The master was angry with this lazy man and dismissed him.

So it is, said Jesus, with the word of God. Some shall take it and use it profitably. Others will do nothing and gain nothing in the end.

Jesus considered God's teachings more important than everyday affairs. One day, he visited Martha and Mary, the sisters of Lazarus, who had been raised from the dead. They were preparing a feast to celebrate the great event. When Jesus entered the house, Mary would not leave his side, for she was anxious to hear his teachings. Her sister Martha, however, bustled around with her pots and pans. Finally, she went up to Jesus and said:

"**Lord**, it isn't fair that my sister Mary sits here and doesn't help with the housework. Tell her that she must help."

But Jesus smiled. "Martha, Martha," he said, "you can do housework every day, but how often is it that I come to your home with the word of God? Mary knows this. She has chosen the better part, and she will be rewarded."

Jesus told many other parables. In some of them, he compared himself to the Good Shepherd who will go any distance to save one lamb who has gone astray. Furthermore, said Jesus, the Good Shepherd is willing to lay down his life to save his sheep. This, too, Jesus was prepared to do.

32.

JESUS PREPARES TO VISIT JERUSALEM

SINCE THE PASSOVER FEAST was soon to be celebrated, Jesus and his disciples made plans to visit Jerusalem, so that they might worship in the Temple. In his heart, Jesus knew that he would die in Jerusalem, as the prophets had predicted. But his destiny was meant to be fulfilled; and he approached the final journey with great serenity.

While passing through Samaria, on the way to Jerusalem, Jesus continued his preaching and healing. At one village, ten unfortunate lepers waited at the crossroads, hoping to be healed. When they saw Jesus they rushed forward and fell on their knees. The crowd drew back, for leprosy was considered to be contagious. But Jesus knew no fear. He lifted his hands over the lepers' heads, and they were healed. Only one of the cured men remained kneeling in thanks. Jesus was very pleased, for this man was a Samaritan, not a Jew. Now, even the Samaritans believed in Jesus and his miracles.

While passing through the town of Jericho, Jesus once again proved that all men might receive salvation through his teachings, even unpopular tax collectors.

Zaccheus was the richest man in Jericho—and the chief tax collector. He was a small, unattractive person, neither better nor worse than anybody else. He was also a determined man. When he heard that Jesus, the famous prophet, was coming to town, he wanted to catch a glimpse of him. Eagerly he left his money bags and rushed out into the crowd. But, being small, Zaccheus couldn't see a thing. So he climbed a sycamore tree and sat there right over the place where Jesus passed.

"Make haste, Zaccheus," called Jesus, seeing the man in the tree, "I will stay at your house while I am in Jericho."

Everyone was surprised to see Jesus enter the home of the tiny tax collector. But Zaccheus was overjoyed. To celebrate his salvation, he gave half his money to the poor and became a devoted follower of Jesus.

After Jericho, Jesus passed through Bethany, his last stop before entering Jerusalem. There, in Bethany, he visited Martha and Mary and their brother Lazarus, who had been raised from the dead. It was the Saturday before the feast of Passover. For the next few days, Jesus would pass from triumph to death, and, then, to glory. The story of his last week in Jerusalem is sometimes known as the *Passion of the Lord.*

33.

THE FATE OF JOHN THE BAPTIST

WHILE JESUS WAS PREPARING to enter Jerusalem, John the Baptist lay in chains deep in the dungeon of King Herod's palace. From the depths of his cell, he continued to preach the coming of the Lord and Saviour. Occasionally, his followers managed to get a message to him, and they told him of Jesus and his wonderful work.

King Herod feared John the Baptist, and was content to keep him in prison without doing him further harm. But Herod's wife, Queen Herodias, was wicked and sinful. Because John had spoken against her, she wished him dead.

One night, during a birthday feast for the king, Herodias introduced her beautiful daughter, Salome. King Herod was delighted, and wished the maiden to dance for him. He promised to award her anything her heart desired, even half his kingdom, if she would perform.

Salome agreed, and danced before the king and his guests. When she finished, Herod said:

"Now, tell me. What do you wish?"

Salome went to her mother, Herodias, for advice. Then she returned to Herod with a terrible request.

"Give me the head of John the Baptist on a silver platter," she demanded.

Herod was shocked. He tried to talk Salome out of her request, promising her jewels and great wealth. But Herodias' daughter insisted. Finally, the king reluctantly gave in, and the great prophet John was slain in the dungeon.

When the followers of Jesus heard this news, they were afraid for

The Beheading of
John the Baptist
Drawing

their Master, for the whole city of Jerusalem was seething with unrest. Everywhere, Roman soldiers were stationed, prepared to quell any riot that might begin because of the Baptist's death. In the Temple, the Pharisees and Sadducees, sworn enemies of Jesus, were plotting ways of doing him harm. Ever since Lazarus had been raised from the dead, they had feared Jesus' power and popularity. Thus, hatred and trouble were brewing in Jerusalem while Jesus prepared to make his entry.

But there were great expectations as well, for the humble Jews of the city looked forward to seeing the great Master from Nazareth. His reputation had spread in spite of his enemies' greatest efforts.

34.

THE CELEBRATION OF THE PALMS

AT A PLACE called the Mount of Olives, Jesus gathered his disciples. He told them that his visit to Jerusalem would be a time of fulfillment of all the ancient prophecies. In accordance with these prophecies, Jesus sent two of his men into the village nearby in order to fetch a spotless white colt that had never been ridden. The prophets had said that the Messiah would one day enter Jerusalem astride a perfect white colt.

In due time, the disciples found such an animal and brought it to the Mount of Olives. There, Jesus mounted the colt and began the journey into Jerusalem. As he passed through the villages outside the city's walls, his disciples cried out:

"Behold the King that cometh in the name of the Lord!"

The Pharisees hearing this were alarmed. They feared a violent revolution that would make Jesus king, for they didn't understand the spiritual meaning of the word. Angrily, they cried to Jesus:

"Make your disciples stop all this shouting."

But Jesus replied:

"If these people are silent, then the stones will cry out—for my message must be heard."

Finally the procession approached the city gates. When Jesus beheld Jerusalem, the great city of the Jews, he began to weep silently, for he knew the destruction and sorrow that would someday befall every house and stone within. But then his heart was made glad, for the multitudes came out in throngs to greet him, laying their cloaks on the road in his path. Many climbed trees for a better view, and others plucked palm leaves from the trees to wave at the Lord. Thus, the first Palm Sunday was celebrated in Jerusalem amid cries of "Hosanna"—which means "Salvation"—and amid great rejoicing.

At twilight, Jesus and his disciples returned on foot to Bethany. The first day had ended in triumph.

35.

THE CLEANSING OF THE TEMPLE

ON THE DAY following his triumphal entry, Jesus returned with his disciples to Jerusalem and went directly to the Temple. In ancient times, it was the custom to erect stalls alongside the Temple's walls for the purposes of selling food and objects for the sacrifice. Gradually, many merchants moved onto the Temple grounds themselves, and conducted their business in sight of the main altar.

Money lenders and changers also set up tables in the Temple, where they conducted themselves in a generally noisy and ungodly manner. Jesus knew about these outrages, but this did not soothe his anger. With a whip in his hands, he rushed into the midst of the money lenders and overturned their tables and stalls, crying:

"The House of God shall be a house of prayer, not a den of thieves!"

Hastily, the merchants and money lenders retreated, but they were not soon to forget this incident. A few days later, many of them were on hand to condemn Jesus to death.

When the defilers were out of the Temple, the poor, the lame, and the blind came before Jesus, and they were miraculously healed. The priests who watched in amazement would not admit Jesus' greatness, fearing to lose their own high status in the city. In fact, they stepped forward and challenged Jesus, demanding to know who he was and by what authority he spoke. As they were speaking, a group of children entered the Temple grounds singing:

"Hosanna to the Son of David, the Messiah."

Jesus turned to the priests and said:

"You asked who I was? Out of the mouths of babes will you hear it."

Christ Driving
the Money-Changers
from the Temple
Etching

Christ Healing the Sick
("The Hundred Guilder Print")
Etching

Christ Preaching
("La Petite Tombe")
Etching

36.

PARABLES AND EVENTS IN THE TEMPLE

AFTER CHASING the money changers and healing the sick, Jesus continued to preach in the Temple. As a teacher, or rabbi, he was entitled to do so, even though the priests and rulers of the city challenged him and wished him away. They were very cautious about causing a riot, however. Many people had gathered in the Temple to hear Jesus, and, if the soldiers had arrested him or stoned him, hundreds would have risen to his defense. So the wicked men merely tried to make Jesus look foolish in the sight of his followers.

One of them held up a coin and asked a treacherous question.

"Since you tell us to pay homage only to God," he asked, "should we continue to pay taxes to Rome?"

Jesus knew this question was an attempt to entangle him. If he said, "Don't pay taxes to Rome," he would surely be arrested. If he seemed to be fearful of Roman authority, then he would appear cowardly and weak. With perfect control, Jesus asked the man to show him the coin. The man complied.

"Whose picture is this on the coin?" asked Jesus.

"That is Caesar," the questioner replied.

"Very well," said Jesus. "Give this to Caesar, since it is his, but give unto God the things that are God's."

Properly rebuked, the troublemakers left the Temple.

On the following day, Jesus came to preach again. This time, many Pharisees and priests assembled to challenge him and interrupt his work.

The Tribute Money
Oil on panel

"Woe unto you, scribes and Pharisees!" he called to them. "You exalt yourselves on earth, but you will be as nothing in the Kingdom of God. Even this great city of Jerusalem will one day fall to ruin; and this Temple, by which you swear, it shall crumble again, because you have based your values on material things and not on God."

The mighty rulers of the city were angered.

"This man says he is the Saviour, the Christ," they said. "But he is just a teacher from Nazareth—and no prophets ever came from Nazareth!"

Patiently, Jesus urged the sinners to repent. There was always room at God's table for the penitent, he said. Then he told the parable of *The Wedding Guest.*

A rich man once held a feast to celebrate his son's wedding. For selfish reasons, those invited failed to come. The rich man was upset, for he had prepared much food and gone to great trouble. After a while, he called his servants and told them to remind his guests of the feast. But the wicked people killed the servants rather than leave their businesses and their other tasks. Fortunately, the king of the city heard about this crime, and sent his army to arrest the murderers.

The rich man then decided to open his doors to anyone who wished to attend the celebration, and he ordered his servants to go out into the streets and invite all those at hand. Many poor and hungry people eagerly came to the feast, first dressing in their best garments as a sign of respect. One man, however, was too eager. He did not bother to change his clothing or to cleanse himself before the meal. He was forcibly made to leave.

Jesus explained his story thus: The Kingdom of God is like the feast; it is there waiting for everyone. Some people will be foolish, and refuse God's invitation to attend. Others, humble though they might be, will accept and enjoy the bounty of Heaven. Still others will be unpre-

The Parable of the
Unworthy Wedding Guest
Drawing

pared, like the man who was not properly dressed. They will be cast out of Heaven.

Another parable had a similar message. It was called *The Foolish and Wise Virgins:*

Ten young ladies were supposed to accompany a bridal party on its way to the Temple. Each girl had a small oil lamp, which was to be lit at the proper time so that the procession would appear festive and beautiful. The bridegroom was detained in arriving, so the maidens sat patiently by the side of the road awaiting him. The hour grew late, and they all fell asleep. About midnight a cry was heard:

"Get ready; the bridegroom is coming!"

The girls hastily prepared themselves. But five of them suddenly discovered that they had forgotten to put oil in their lamps. Nervously, they asked their wiser friends to lend them some oil. But the others needed every drop, and advised the foolish virgins to hasten and purchase the oil they needed. Then the wise maidens lit their lamps and went forth to greet the bridal party.

The foolish girls ran all over town, seeking oil. But the hour was late, and none was to be found. Finally, when they returned to the wedding feast, the doors of the house were locked, and they could not enter.

So it is with the Kingdom of God, said Jesus. God's call may come at any moment, even while you are asleep; therefore, always be ready, or you may not be able to enter the Kingdom of Heaven.

Jesus then prophesied many strange and wonderful things that would happen in the future. He spoke until evening approached; then he prepared to leave the Temple. At the door of the building, there was the customary poor box. Jesus paused and watched as the rich men of Jerusalem dropped in large sums of money to impress their neighbors.

When they were gone, a poor widow approached the box and deposited the sum of two mites, or one penny. Jesus turned to his friends and said:

"For all the wealth of the rich, God will appreciate this poor woman's gift many times over, for the rich will never miss what they gave. But this poor woman gave all she owned."

So saying, Jesus and his friends left the Temple of Jerusalem for the very last time.

37.

THE PLOT AGAINST JESUS

IT WAS WEDNESDAY of the final week. Jesus and his disciples decided to preach in the city and in the villages nearby. As they walked
from Bethany, the group passed a withered fig tree. Peter was surprised.
He remembered having seen that same tree standing tall and straight
only the day before.

Peter soon learned that Jesus had cursed the fig tree so that it
withered. On Monday, Jesus had been hungry, and when he approached
the tree in order to eat some figs, he found that it was bare. Jesus did not
mean to be vengeful toward a harmless fig tree. But he wanted to teach
his disciples a lesson.

"When the word of God comes to you and you are bare as that fig
tree," said Jesus, "then you will also wither."

Peter was nonetheless amazed that the tree had withered so fast.

"Have faith," said Jesus. "Faith can move mountains and fulfill all
righteous desires. There is nothing like faith in God. He will feed you
when you are hungry, and give you drink when you are thirsty. All these
things can be accomplished by faith."

In the evening, Jesus and his followers returned to Bethany. But
one disciple was missing—unnoticed by the rest. He was Judas Iscariot,
a quiet, brooding man, who had remained behind in Jerusalem to take
part in a terrible plot against Jesus.

38.

JUDAS ISCARIOT

IT WAS DARK in the city. Judas crept along the narrow streets until
he found the house of Caiaphas, a high priest of the Temple and the

enemy of Jesus. In Caiaphas' room, several men were planning to capture Jesus so that they might turn him over to the Roman authorities.

They had to be careful. If they arrested Jesus while he was preaching, a riot might result. Therefore, it was best to take him by surprise when he was alone. Caiaphas turned to Judas:

"When would be the best time to capture your Master?"

Judas was trembling and worried.

"First you must tell me what I will get if I betray him," he said.

"The price is thirty pieces of silver," answered Caiaphas, "the same price you would get for selling a slave. But it is a good price."

After a moment, Judas accepted the deal. He told the conspirators that Jesus frequently prayed alone in the garden of Gethsemane and that he would be an easy victim at such a time.

"I shall be nearby," Judas continued. "In case you don't recognize the Nazarene, I will go up to him and kiss him on the cheek. That will be your signal."

Caiaphas was pleased, and told Judas to return to his friends. Judas left the room thinking that the priests merely wanted to arrest Jesus. He did not know that they planned to accuse him of treason against Caesar and thereby enable the Roman authorities to nail him to a cross until he was dead. The priests and Pharisees had no power to put a man to death; that power rested with Pontius Pilate, the Roman governor of Jerusalem. But the priests did have the power to bring charges against anyone they chose.

Jesus knew what was about to happen. Once again, he told his followers that he would be crucified in Jerusalem, and that, three days later, he would rise from the dead, for he was Christ, the Messiah, and it was his destiny to be sacrificed. Centuries before, Moses had commanded his people to sacrifice a paschal lamb and place its blood on their doorposts, so that the Angel of Death would pass over them and they would be spared. Now, Jesus would give his life on earth, so that all mankind, believing in him as the Messiah, might be spared the hopelessness of death and be redeemed of all the sins and transgressions of the world.

39.

THE LAST SUPPER

ON THURSDAY, the entire Jewish nation prepared to celebrate the Passover feast, which commemorated the ancient Exodus from Egypt. As religious Jews, Jesus and his disciples sought a place where they might hold the ritual supper. At first, the disciples were worried about finding such a place, but Jesus said:

"In the city, you will see a man carrying a pitcher of water. Follow him. In his house, upstairs, a room will be ready and a table set. We shall hold our supper there."

As Jesus had said, the disciples found a man carrying a pitcher of water; and he led them to a modest house, where the Passover table was set and ready. That evening, Jesus and his twelve disciples, including Judas Iscariot, came into Jerusalem for the meal.

Though it was a joyous holiday, a somber mood seemed to hang over the festivities. The disciples, remembering Jesus' prophecy that he would die in Jerusalem, were sad and concerned. Nevertheless, they gathered around the table and began talking quietly among themselves. Soon a slight argument began.

"What is wrong?" asked Jesus.

One of the men replied:

"We should like to know which of us you favor most and which one will be most highly exalted in Heaven?"

Once before, the disciples had wondered about this and, at that time, Jesus had said:

"He who wishes to be first in heaven must be last on earth."

Now, as a demonstration, Jesus removed his outer cloak, filled a basin with water, and knelt down before Peter.

Christ Washing
the Disciples' Feet
Drawing

The Last Supper
*Drawing after
Leonardo da Vinci*

"Let me wash your feet," he said.

Peter was amazed. How could the Lord perform such a humble service?

"Please rise, my Lord," insisted Peter.

But Jesus explained:

"When I wash your feet, you become a part of me."

Peter reflected.

"If that is true," he said, "then wash not only my feet but also my hands and my head."

Jesus was pleased at Peter's devotion and proceeded to wash his feet and the feet of all the other disciples. Then Jesus resumed his place at the table and said,

"Now you are clean; all but one of you. For one of you will betray me."

These words fell like thunder on the ears of the disciples. Nervously, each one asked:

"Is it I, Lord?"

Jesus did not immediately reply. Instead, he dipped some meat into a bowl of herbs and vinegar and passed it to Judas Iscariot as a sign of his knowledge that Judas would betray him. The others did not seem to understand this, and they remained perplexed and uneasy. Then Jesus turned to the deceitful Iscariot and said to him:

179

"What you must do, go and do quickly!"

Judas immediately rose from the table and fearfully left the room. The others thought that he had been sent on an errand, since Judas often handled finances for the group. They did not question Jesus any further, nor did he tell them that Judas would betray him as part of God's great plan.

Instead, Jesus rose, lifted a piece of the unleavened bread in his hand, and said:

"Take this bread, which I have blessed, and eat it, for it is my body."

Then he took a cup of wine, blessed it and said:

"This is my blood of the new testament, which is shed for many in the remission of sins."

The disciples knew that they were witnessing a sacred act, and they knelt, and each received a piece of bread and a sip of wine in communion with Jesus. Then he said to them:

"I will not drink wine again until I drink it with God, my Father, in Heaven."

And, as they rose, he further announced:

"A new commandment I give unto you: Love one another as I love you—and all men will know that you are my disciples."

Thus, the first Communion was performed in a modest room in Jerusalem.

40.

THE AGONY IN THE GARDEN

AFTER THE MEAL, the disciples sang a hymn and went out into the streets. They headed for the Mount of Olives, where it was Jesus' habit to pray alone. As they walked, Jesus turned to Peter and said:

"When I am gone, I fear my disciples will flee."

"Not I," Peter exclaimed. "I would go to prison and even to death for my Lord."

But Jesus knew the weakness of men.

"Peter," he said, "before the cock crows twice, before the morning comes, you will deny me three times and say you never knew me."

Peter was amazed and protested. Indeed, all the disciples pledged anew their undying faith. Jesus said nothing more. He walked into the quiet garden of Gethsemane on the Mount of Olives. There he signaled Peter, James, and John to follow him and keep guard while he prayed. Jesus felt sorrowful and uneasy. Kneeling alone in the darkness, he experienced the fear and terror common to all mankind, and he called out to God:

"Father, if it is possible that I might be spared the suffering and the pain that I know will come, let me be spared. But if I must suffer as part of Your plan, let it be done. I am ready."

And, as he prayed thus, an angel appeared above him, holding forth a cup of comfort. But Jesus knew no comfort. His agony was so great that large drops of blood fell from his face. Then he seemed to swoon. When he regained his strength, the fear and terror passed away. He rose and returned, calm and unafraid, to Peter, John, and James.

Unfortunately, the three disciples had fallen asleep while they waited for their Master.

"Could you not watch even one short hour?" Jesus asked them as they awakened.

The men were embarrassed, and tried to make excuses.

"I know," said Jesus. "The spirit was ready, but the flesh is weak."

Then he asked them to watch again while he returned to his prayers. At the same moment, led by Judas Iscariot and the high priests of the Temple, a group of Roman soldiers entered the garden.

Quietly, their swords drawn, they stationed themselves behind trees, waiting for the signal from Judas.

The Agony in
the Garden
Etching

Christ Awakening
the Apostles on
the Mount of Olives
Drawing

The Arrest
of Christ
Drawing

41.

THE ARREST

JESUS ROSE from his prayers, ready to enact God's plan. As he turned to walk from the garden, Judas came up alongside him.

"Hail, Master," he said in a friendly voice. Then holding his torch close to Jesus, he leaned over and kissed him on the cheek. Jesus understood. Quietly, he said to Judas:

"So, you have chosen to betray me with a kiss."

No sooner had he spoken, when a dozen Roman soldiers led by a priest surrounded him, their swords in the air. Angrily, the disciples jumped to their feet and attacked the soldiers. But Jesus cried out:

"Put up your weapons, for all those who live by the sword shall die by the sword!"

One of the disciples acted hastily and slashed the ear of the priest's servant with his sword. Jesus held him back and gently touched the servant's ear, so that it was cured. The disciples, seeing this, retreated into the shadows as other soldiers and priests came to capture Jesus. Cruelly, the soldiers bound him with ropes and poked him with their spears.

"Am I a common thief," asked Jesus, "that you treat me like this? Only yesterday I preached in the Temple, and you heard me and did not attack me."

But the assailants would not listen. Hurriedly they dragged Jesus from the garden of Gethsemane amid their flickering torches and upraised spears. The fateful prophecy was about to be fulfilled.

42.

JESUS BEFORE THE PRIESTS

WAITING IN JERUSALEM were Caiaphas, the high priest, and his father-in-law, Annas, who was also an official of the Temple. Before these men, Jesus was brought as a prisoner to answer charges.

First, Caiaphas asked Jesus about his disciples and his doctrine. Jesus answered that he had never preached secretly or maliciously.

"I spoke openly to the world and in the Temple as a good Jew," he said. "You know this, your people have seen me."

Caiaphas was not pleased with this answer. He signaled one of the soldiers to strike Jesus across the face.

"Why do you strike me?" asked Jesus quietly. "If I have spoken evil, God will strike me, not you."

Outside in the courtyard of Caiaphas' house, Peter waited nervously in the shadows. He had followed the band of soldiers that had captured Jesus, and he was anxious and afraid. While he waited some men built a fire since it was cold in the morning air. As Peter moved close to warm his hands a young woman saw him and said:

"This fellow was with the prophet Jesus who is now a prisoner."

Peter was alarmed.

"That's not so," he said. "I don't even know that man."

Another person looked up.

"Oh, yes," he said, "you were one of his followers."

"No," Peter insisted. "I never heard of Jesus before tonight."

The first girl laughed.

"Don't fool us. You are his disciple. Come on, tell us what he's like."

The Denial
of Peter
Oil on canvas

Christ Before Annas
Drawing

The Repentant Peter
Etching

Peter became angry. Again he denied ever knowing Jesus or being part of his band. Then, suddenly in the distance, the cock crowed in the dawn. A cold chill ran over Peter's skin as he remembered Jesus' prophecy, *Before the cock crows, you will deny me three times.*

Horrified at his weakness and disloyalty, Peter burst into tears and rushed from the scene.

Inside Caiaphas' house, the long questioning of Jesus continued. Many witnesses were brought in to testify against the man from Nazareth. Some of them were paid to lie; others purposely misinterpreted what Jesus had said, so that it might be used against him. Throughout, Jesus made no reply.

Finally Caiaphas rose and pointing his finger at Jesus, he demanded:

"Are you Christ, the Messiah, the Son of God?"

Jesus replied very simply.

"You have spoken the truth," he said.

This was too much for the high priest. Shouting "blasphemy," he turned to his council of priests,

"You have heard this blasphemy against God," he cried. "It is a sin to call oneself the Messiah; and such a sin must be punished by death. What is your decision?"

The council dared not go against Caiaphas' wishes. Without further discussion, they condemned Jesus and ordered him taken to the Roman governor, for they had no authority to put him to death. The soldiers grabbed Jesus by the arms and took him out into the street. Once alone with him, they began to punch him and spit in his face, laughing all the while and saying:

"If you're the Messiah, tell us which of us hit you and spat in your face."

Jesus did not reply. He bowed his head in prayer as they led him away.

Watching from the shadows was Judas Iscariot, who had come to Caiaphas' house to get his thirty pieces of silver. Now he saw Jesus being led away, bound and disgraced. He knew the Romans would put his Master to death and he said to himself:

"My God, what have I done?"

184

Judas Returning
the Thirty Pieces
of Silver
Oil on wood

Trembling, he took the money and returned it to Caiaphas.

"I have sinned and betrayed a righteous man," he cried. "Take back this blood money; I'll have no part of it."

Then Judas ran from the scene to his house where he took his own life by hanging.

The priests did not want his money, for they knew it was accursed. So they took it and purchased a plot of land owned by a potter. Here the poor and unknown of the city were buried free of charge. Today such places are known as Potter's Fields—lonely memorials to the treacherous Judas Iscariot.

43.

THE TRIAL BEFORE PONTIUS PILATE

IT WAS EARLY Friday morning. Bound and guarded, Jesus was led to the palace of Pontius Pilate, the Roman governor of Jerusalem. Many of Jesus' enemies lurked outside the palace, waiting for news of what was happening.

Pilate sat on his throne surrounded by his soldiers. Before him were the representatives of the high priests.

"What charges do you bring against this man?" asked the governor.

The priests stated their case, saying that Jesus had spoken against Caesar and that he had corrupted the people with false teachings. Pilate

Christ Before Pilate
Oil on canvas

185

Christ Before Pilate
Etching

looked over the bill of complaints that the priests had submitted. Then he summoned Jesus before him.

"Are you the King of the Jews?" he asked.

Jesus answered very quietly.

"Yes," he said, "but my kingdom is not of this world, but of the world hereafter."

Pilate was hesitant. Assuming that the complaints were religious, not political, he turned to the priests and said:

"I find no fault in this man."

The priests were emphatic. They continued to demand action from Pilate, for the law gave them no power to put Jesus to death.

"This man has corrupted the entire nation," they said, "all the way from Galilee to Jerusalem."

When Pilate heard mention of Galilee, he decided to unburden the case on King Herod, who was responsible for order in Galilee, and he ordered Jesus taken to Herod's palace in Jerusalem.

For a long time, King Herod had been quarreling with the Roman authorities. When Jesus came before him, he hardly knew what to do.

"Can you perform some miracles for me?" asked the foolish king.

Jesus was silent. Outraged by this indifference, Herod, in mockery, ordered Jesus dressed up in gaudy robes, as would befit a comic "king." But he did not want to take responsibility for Jesus' death. So he ordered:

"Send him back to Pilate, and let the Romans handle him."

And so Jesus returned to the Roman governor. He was questioned again and again. For hours, Pilate listened to the arguments of the priests, and he became bored and short-tempered.

"I will have this man whipped," he said. "Then we will release him with a warning. That should satisfy you."

But the priests would not be satisfied. Pilate had a new idea. It was the custom during Passover for one prisoner to be freed upon the people's request. Pilate thought that the crowds would ask for Jesus, since he was not a murderer or a robber like the other prisoners. But Jesus' enemies had gathered in that crowd—all the merchants and Pharisees—and, when Pilate asked them which prisoner they wanted released, they called, "Barabbas! Barabbas!" although Barabbas was a common thief.

While Pilate was trying to resolve his dilemma, his wife came to him. She had dreamed about Jesus and believed him innocent of all the charges made by the priests. She urged her husband to release him.

Pilate went before the crowd and asked:

"Do you want me to crucify this man just because he called himself King of the Jews? This is hardly a crime."

But the people continued to shout for the release of Barabbas. Pilate was annoyed. He had other things to do, so he took a basin of water and poured it over his hands.

"I wash my hands of this matter," he cried to the crowd, "because I find no fault in this man."

Nevertheless to please the mob, he freed Barabbas the robber, and had Jesus flogged. Then he ordered his soldiers to dress Jesus in an old

Christ at
the Column
Oil on canvas

Pilate Washing
His Hands
Oil on canvas

The Mocking
of Christ
Drawing

Ecce Homo
("Christ Before
the People")
Etching

purple robe, such as a king might have worn, and crown him with a wreath of thorns. The soldiers enjoyed this cruel sport, and they hit Jesus and spat in his face as they dressed him.

Finally Pilate brought Jesus out into the courtyard before the mob.

"Here is the man," he said. "For the last time, what shall I do with him?"

Jesus' enemies shouted:

"Crucify him! Crucify him!"

Pilate turned to Jesus, and urged him to say something, or do something that could appease the crowd. But Jesus knew that it was his destiny to die, and he said to Pilate,

"It is not in your hands, for you have no power except the power given to you by God."

Pilate then called the priests from the crowd. Once more, he argued with them, trying to avoid responsibility for Jesus' death. But the crafty priests said:

"He has called himself a king. There is only one king and that is Caesar. Any man allowing him to live is no friend of Caesar's, as Caesar will learn."

Hearing this very meaningful threat, Pilate no longer argued. He turned to the mob and announced:

"Behold your king!"

The people shouted:

"We have no king but Caesar."

"Very well," said Pilate—and he sentenced Jesus to be crucified.

44.

THE CRUCIFIXION OF JESUS

BEYOND THE WALLS of Jerusalem was a hill called Golgotha. There condemned prisoners were crucified upon great wooden crosses, and their bodies tossed into a pit. To this place Jesus of Nazareth came, dragging a heavy wooden cross upon his back while Roman soldiers led the way.

By now, it was midday, and many of the poor and common people of Jerusalem were out on the streets and in the markets. They could see the sorrowful procession of prisoners, weighed down under heavy beams of wood, heading toward Golgotha. Many recognized Jesus, the kindly teacher from Galilee, and they left their work to follow, weeping to see Jesus burdened by the heavy cross, an ugly crown of thorns on his head and the wounds of his whipping still fresh upon his skin. But Jesus turned to them, in his agony, and said:

"Do not weep for me, but for yourselves and your children. For, behold, evil days are coming to Jerusalem."

Then he faltered under the weight of the cross, and he fell, and lay in the gutter. The soldiers ordered a man named Simon of Cyrene to lift the cross, so that Jesus might continue his final journey. So it was that Jesus, falling and in agony, reached the pinnacle of Golgotha.

Now it was time for the cruel execution. The soldiers disrobed Jesus and flung his garments to the ground. There, others grabbed up his seamless robe and began rolling dice to see which one should claim it.

Christ Carrying the Cross
Drawing

The Raising of the Cross
Drawing

The Raising of the Cross
Oil on canvas

All this they did as Jesus was nailed by his hands and feet to the beams of the cross. He neither struggled nor cried out. But he lifted his eyes toward Heaven, and exclaimed:

"Forgive them, Father, for they know not what they do."

Then the soldiers fastened to the topmost beam of the cross a sign that read *Jesus of Nazareth, King of the Jews*. It was meant in mockery.

Once this was done, they raised Jesus on his cross to an upright position, so that he hung most painfully above the ground by the nails in his hands and in his feet.

Below, many scornful people watched this execution, calling to Jesus:

"If you are the Son of God, then save yourself and come down from the cross."

But Jesus knew his destiny. He had even refused to drink a potion that might have numbed his pain, knowing that he had to suffer for the sins of the world. And so he looked out across the city of Jerusalem in prayer, while the crowd taunted him from below.

Then he turned his eyes to the left and to the right, where two other prisoners were nailed to crosses. Both were thieves and feared death, and one of them cried to him:

"If you are the Christ, save us from this torture."

But the other said:

"If you are the Christ, remember me when you enter into Heaven." And Jesus promised to remember him.

Now, also, in the crowd at the foot of the cross, stood Mary, Jesus' mother, Mary, the mother of James, and a third Mary, who was Mary Magdalene. Some of the disciples had come there as well, fearfully and

Christ Crucified
Between the Two Thieves
("The Three Crosses")
Etching

Calvary
Drawing

The Crucifixion
Oil on wood

in sorrow. When Jesus saw his mother and his friends, his heart was very heavy, and he whispered to the disciple John:

"Take care of my mother when I am dead."

Then a strange darkness began to fall over the city, though it was early in the afternoon; and Jesus lifted his head toward Heaven, and cried in pain:

"My God, my God, why hast Thou forsaken me?"

Feeling pity, someone raised a wet sponge to Jesus' lips so that he might have some small relief. But it was too late for comfort.

"Into Thy hands I commend my spirit," cried Jesus, the man from Nazareth, and he departed his earthly life and died.

At this dark moment, the sky became pitch black. Buildings trembled, and the graveyards gave up their dead. Even the veil that hung before the Holy of Holies in the Temple suddenly tore in two, as though rent by invisible hands, and the air seemed filled with moans and crying, so that many who had scorned and mocked Jesus as he died fell on their knees and cried out:

"Truly, this was the Son of God!"

191

Christ Crucified
Between the Two Thieves:
Christ Offered a Sponge
Drawing

The Crucifixion:
The Blow of the Lance
Drawing

45.

THE BURIAL

A KINDLY JEW named Joseph of Arimathea had often heard Jesus preach and been impressed with what he had heard. This man wished to claim Jesus' body, so that he might give it decent burial.

The hour was late and the Sabbath was approaching. By Jewish law, it was forbidden to bury anyone on the Sabbath, so Joseph hurried to Pilate, the governor, to request permission to remove Jesus from the cross. At first, Pilate wished to leave Jesus there, in humiliation. But Joseph would not be dissuaded, and, finally, the Roman governor granted his wish.

The Descent from
the Cross:
Removal of the Nails
Etching

The Descent from
the Cross
Etching

The Descent from
the Cross
Oil on panel

The Lamentation
over Christ
Drawing

Lamentation
Drawing

Christ Carried
to the Tomb
Etching

The Entombment
Drawing

The Entombment
Oil on canvas

Joseph then hurried to Golgotha. As he watched, a Roman centurion pierced Jesus' side with a spear to make sure he was dead. Then they removed his body from the cross.

Carefully, Joseph wrapped Jesus in fine linen. With the aid of the sorrowing disciples, he carried the body to his home, where there was a garden. In this garden was a cave, prepared especially for burials. Here Joseph wished to bury Jesus, but, first, he called the three Marys to his side, and, together, they anointed Jesus' body with fine oils and spices. Then, with reverence and sorrow, they buried him.

In Jerusalem, the Pharisees and the priests came before Pilate and said:

"This man Jesus boasted that he would rise from the dead on the third day after his death. We must make sure that his disciples do not steal his body away and then pretend that he is risen from the grave."

"What do you want me to do?" asked Pilate.

"Place a guard at the tomb," they answered, "and roll a heavy stone before the opening, so that it is sealed. Then his disciples will be helpless."

Pilate agreed, and sent three soldiers to watch at the grave, where an enormous boulder was rolled in front of the opening. Then the Sabbath came and the city was quiet. Jesus' ordeal had ended.

46.

THE RESURRECTION

ON SUNDAY MORNING, Mary the mother of Jesus, Mary the mother of James, and Mary Magdalene came to the garden where Jesus was buried, wishing to pay him final homage. As they approached the tomb, they saw an astounding sight. The Roman soldiers had vanished; the great boulder that had been set against the opening of the grave was now rolled away down the path; and a glorious angel, all dressed in white, sat at the entrance to the tomb.

"Fear not," said the angel to the women. "Jesus of Nazareth, whom you seek, has risen from the grave as he promised, and will shortly go to Galilee and appear before his followers."

Then the angel pointed inside the tomb where the women had seen

The Resurrection
Oil on canvas

Christ Appears
to Mary Magdalene
Oil on canvas

Christ as a Gardener
("Noli Me Tangere")
Drawing

Jesus laid to rest. Now, there was his empty shroud, and nothing more. The women were stunned. What could they believe? Had someone come and stolen Jesus' body? Mary Magdalene began to weep, and started down the path toward the city. Suddenly, she saw a shadowy figure of a man in the road.

"Why are you weeping?" asked the man.

Magdalene lowered her head to hide her tears, and she replied:

"I believe that someone has stolen the body of my Lord."

"Look at me," said the man. "Don't you know my face?"

Magdalene looked up to see Jesus standing before her, his face radiant and serene. The amazed woman reached out to touch him, for she could not believe her eyes. But Jesus withdrew, and said:

"Do not touch me now, for I have not yet ascended to Heaven."

Then he vanished.

Joyously, Magdalene ran back to the garden where Peter and John had come to behold the empty tomb. She told them what she had seen. But they were baffled and confused by her story.

In the city, word spread that Jesus of Nazareth had disappeared from his tomb and was actually risen from the dead. Many disbelieving persons said that his body had been stolen and hidden by his followers. But others believed in the resurrection, and took great encouragement from the news. Thus dawned the first Easter Sunday amid doubt and hope, for as Jesus had said earlier that week:

"Destroy this temple of my body,
and in three days I will raise it up."

47.

JESUS AT EMMAUS

Christ on
the Road to Emmaus
Drawing

Christ at Emmaus
Oil on panel

TWO MEN FROM THE CITY of Emmaus heard the news about Jesus' resurrection. They staunchly believed that he had risen from the dead and was the Saviour promised by the prophets of old. As they walked upon the road toward their home, they spoke of the events in Jerusalem, bemoaning the tragic death of the kindly teacher from Galilee.

As they were talking, another man, a stranger, joined them and entered into the conversation.

"What has happened?" the stranger asked.

Cleophas, one of the first two men, told the story of how Jesus had been cruelly tortured and crucified.

"But," he added, "Jesus also rose from the dead this very day, as he promised, for he was a great and wonderful prophet."

The stranger, seeing that Cleophas and his friend were greatly upset over Jesus' death, spoke to them with words of profound meaning.

"You must understand," he said, "that it was Jesus' destiny to suffer, according to what the prophets of old have taught us. That is why he will enter into glory."

The men from Emmaus were strongly impressed by the stranger and invited him to their home to share their evening meal.

"Abide with us," they said, "for evening fast approaches."

All three then went to the house of Cleophas. There a loaf of bread was placed before the stranger, so that he might have the honor of blessing it. This he did, and, when he raised his hands, suddenly the men saw that it was Jesus Christ, the Messiah, who had walked with them along the road and now sat at their table. As they looked on in amazement, Jesus vanished from sight.

Joyously, and in haste, Cleophas and his friends rushed back to Jerusalem to spread the word that Jesus had truly reappeared.

48.

JESUS APPEARS TO HIS DISCIPLES

THE DISCIPLES HEARD the good news from Emmaus. They were overjoyed and yet afraid, — Jerusalem had become a dangerous place for Jesus' followers. For this reason, they hid themselves in a small room in a friendly house. Here they spoke of the wonders of the resurrection.

As they talked, Jesus himself suddenly appeared in their midst and said to them:

"Peace be with you."

The disciples were overwhelmed. Was this a spirit or was it really their beloved Master risen from the dead? Jesus sensed their doubts.

"Look at my hands and see the marks of the nails that pierced them," he said. "Look at my chest, where the spear was thrust. Have you not read the Scriptures that predicted these events?"

The disciples were ashamed of their doubts, and they fell down before Jesus in prayer. He blessed them and instructed them in their tasks. Then he asked for some food, and they served him broiled fish and honey.

When he had finished eating, Jesus comforted his disciples once again.

"It was necessary for me to suffer," he said, "so that I might relieve the world of its sins."

49.

DOUBTING THOMAS

AFTER JESUS LEFT HIS DISCIPLES, Thomas came into the room. He had been out on an errand, and had missed seeing his Master. The other men excitedly told him that Jesus had actually appeared and eaten with them in that very room. Thomas would not accept their story.

"Until I can touch him with my own hands," he said, "I will not believe it."

Eight days later, the disciples were gathered in the room again, when Jesus suddenly appeared as before. Thomas was surprised, but still doubtful.

"Come forward," said Jesus. "See my hands and the place where the nail has pierced, and see on my side where I was wounded by the spear. Touch these, so that you will believe."

Thomas went over to Jesus and touched the wound on his side and the hole in each hand where a nail had pierced him on the cross. Then Thomas fell on his knees, exclaiming:

"My Lord and my God, I do believe."

Jesus pointed up a lesson from this incident:

"Thomas is blessed; he believes in me because he has seen me and touched my wounds. But more blessed are they that believe in me, even though they have not seen me."

The Incredulity
of Thomas
Drawing

The Incredulity
of Thomas
Drawing

The Ascension
Oil on canvas

50.

THE ASCENSION

AFTER MANY DAYS, the disciples returned to their homes in Galilee, and took up their old calling as fishermen. They needed time to collect their thoughts and fully appreciate the great tasks that lay ahead.

One day, they all set out in different boats to fish on the Sea of Tiberias. For hours they threw out their nets and lines, but caught nothing. Then Peter saw a man standing on the shore, and at once he recognized Jesus. Overjoyed, he leaped into the water and swam to the beach. The other disciples followed him in their boats.

It was a joyous meeting. With Jesus in their midst, the men found many fish in their nets, for he had performed a miracle as in days past. After they had eaten the fish, they gathered at Jesus' feet to hear his message.

"Go into the world," he said, "and feed my sheep—for all people are like sheep in need of a shepherd. Each one of you has his duty to spread my message and to glorify God in the name of the Father, and of

199

the Son, and of the Holy Spirit." Then he repeated his great commandment:

"Love one another, as I love you."

For forty days, Jesus remained on earth after his resurrection. During this time he met with his disciples and continued to instruct them. One day, he asked them to meet on the Mount of Olives near Jerusalem. There he stood before them for the very last time on earth. Then, lifting his hands in a blessing, he ascended to Heaven and to God amid singing angels and great glory.

Thus ended the earthly life of Jesus, the Saviour, who, as the Lamb of God, had been sacrificed in the remission of sins for all mankind.